Second Workshop on Annotation and Exploitation of Parallel Corpora 2011

(AEPC 2011)

Held with the 8th International Conference on Recent Advances in Natural Language Processing 2011 (RANLP 2011)

Hissar, Bulgaria
15 September 2011

ISBN: 978-1-62276-463-1

Printed from e-media with permission by:

Curran Associates, Inc.
57 Morehouse Lane
Red Hook, NY 12571

Some format issues inherent in the e-media version may also appear in this print version.

Printed by Curran Associates, Inc. (2012)

Association for Computational Linguistics
209 N. Eighth Street
Stroudsburg, Pennsylvania 18360

Phone: 1-570-476-8006
Fax: 1-570-476-0860

acl@aclweb.org

Additional copies of this publication are available from:

Curran Associates, Inc.
57 Morehouse Lane
Red Hook, NY 12571 USA
Phone: 845-758-0400
Fax: 845-758-2634
Email: curran@proceedings.com
Web: www.proceedings.com

Table of Contents

Preface

This workshop is a follow-up of the First Workshop on Annotation and Exploitation of Parallel Corpora (http://math.ut.ee/tlt9/aepc/).

The creation of parallel corpora has been very active especially since 90s. The globalization, the extension of EU with new countries as well as the availability of open-source places for information, such as Wikipedia, DBPeadia, etc. required a multilingual approach towards the interpersonal and official communication. This status quo produced a lot of parallel data – especially administrative and political documents in several languages (EuroParl), but also news (SETIMES) and texts on various topics (wikipedia, bi- and multilingual web sites). However, the fast compilation of large amounts of data very often compromised in lower quality of paralleling texts. Here comes the challenge to discover the inconsistencies in these huge quantities of parallel data, to process them in adequate ways, and to exploit them for various applications: QA, Information Retrieval, Machine Translation, etc. The parallel corpora go beyond word-to-word alignments. They rely on dependency, constituent or semantic pairings. There appeared guidelines and tools for aligning linguistic structures, which raised the issue of transferability of aligning schemes from one language to another, and also for the compatibility among various resources.

The topics, which fall within the scope of the workshop, include: Strategies for creation of annotated parallel corpora; Annotation guidelines for alignment; Annotation alignment transfer over languages; Tools for manual and automatic processing and exploitation of parallel corpora; Problems in manual and automatic alignment; Syntax-based and semantic-based approaches to using parallel corpora in MT; Parallel Grammars; Parallel Statistical Parsing; Usability of the existing parallel resources for various applications.

The workshop has been supported by the European project EuroMatrixPlus – Bringing Machine Translation for European Languages to the User.

The Organizers

Organizers:

Kiril Simov (IICT, Bulgarian Academy of Sciences)
Petya Osenova (Sofia University "St. Kl. Ohridski" and IICT Bulgarian Academy of Sciences)
Radovan Garabik (JÚL'Š, Slovak Academy of Sciences)
Jürg Tiedemann (Uppsala University)

Program Committee:

António Branco (University of Lisbon)
Nicoletta Calzolari (Institute of Computational Linguistics of the National Research Council)
Koenraad De Smedt (University of Bergen)
Dan Flickinger (Stanford University)
Dale Gerdemann (University of Tübingen)
Voula Giouli (Institute for Language and Speech Processing)
Silvia Hansen (University of Mainz)
Erhard Hinrichs (University of Tübingen)
Valia Kordoni (University of Saarland)
Vladislav Kubon (Charles University)
Lothar Lemnitzer (Berlin-Brandenburg Academy of Sciences and Humanities)
Preslav Nakov (National University of Singapore)
Cristina Vertan (University of Hamburg)
Eline Westerhout (University of Utrecht)

Invited Speaker:

Preslav Nakov (National University of Singapore)

Workshop Program

Friday, 16 September 2011

9:20–9:30	Opening
9:30–10:30	*Reusing Parallel Corpora between Related Languages* Preslav Nakov
10:30–11:00	Coffee Break
11:00–11:30	*Discontinuous Constituents: a Problematic Case for Parallel Corpora Annotation and Querying* Marilisa Amoia, Kerstin Kunz and Ekaterina Lapshinova-Koltunski
11:30–12:00	*Parallel Corpora in Aspectual Studies of Non-Aspect Languages* Maria Stambolieva
12:00–12:30	*Coreference Annotator - A new annotation tool for aligned bilingual corpora* Mara Tsoumari and Georgios Petasis
12:30–14:00	Lunch
14:00–14:30	*A tagged and aligned corpus for the study of Proper Names in translation* Emeline Lecuit, Denis Maurel and Duško Vitas
14:30–15:00	*Using Manual and Parallel Aligned Corpora for Machine Translation Services within an On-line Content Management System* Cristina Vertan and Monica Gavrila
15:00–15:30	*Building the multilingual TUT parallel treebank* Manuela Sanguinetti and Cristina Bosco
15:30–16:00	Coffee Break
16:00–16:30	*Bulgarian-English Parallel Treebank: Word and Semantic Level Alignment* Kiril Simov, Petya Osenova, Laska Laskova, Aleksandar Savkov and Stanislava Kancheva
16:30–16:40	Closing Remarks

Reusing Parallel Corpora between Related Languages (invited talk)

Preslav Nakov
National University of Singapore
nakov@comp.nus.edu.sg

Abstract

Recent developments in statistical machine translation (SMT), *e.g.*, the availability of efficient implementations of integrated open-source toolkits like Moses, have made it possible to build a prototype system with decent translation quality for any language pair in a few days or even hours. This is so in theory. In practice, doing so requires having a large set of parallel sentence-aligned bilingual texts (a *bi-text*) for that language pair, which is often unavailable. Large high-quality bi-texts are rare; except for Arabic, Chinese, and some official languages of the European Union (EU), most of the 6,500+ world languages remain resource-poor from an SMT viewpoint. This number is even more striking if we consider language *pairs* instead of individual languages, *e.g.*, while Arabic and Chinese are among the most resource-rich languages for SMT, the Arabic-Chinese language pair is quite resource-poor. Moreover, even resource-rich language pairs could be poor in bi-texts for a specific domain, *e.g.*, biomedical text, conversational text, *etc.*

Due to the increasing volume of EU parliament debates and the ever-growing European legislation, the official languages of the EU are especially privileged from an SMT perspective. While this includes "classic SMT languages" such as English and French (which were already resource-rich), and some important international ones like Spanish and Portuguese, many of the rest have a limited number of speakers and were resource-poor until a few years ago. Thus, becoming an official language of the EU has turned out to be an easy recipe for getting resource-rich in bi-texts quickly.

Our aim is to tap the potential of the EU resources so that they can be used by other non-EU languages that are closely related to one or more official languages of the EU.

We propose to use bi-texts for resource-rich language pairs to build better SMT systems for resource-poor pairs by exploiting the similarity between a resource-poor language and a resource-rich one.

We are motivated by the observation that related languages tend to have (1) similar word order and syntax, and, more importantly, (2) overlapping vocabulary, *e.g.*, *casa* (house) is used in both Spanish and Portuguese; they also have (3) similar spelling. This vocabulary overlap means that the resource-rich auxiliary language can be used as a source of translation options for words that cannot be translated with the resources available for the resource-poor language. In actual text, the vocabulary overlap might extend from individual words to short phrases (especially if the resource-rich languages has been transliterated to look like the resource-poor one), which means that translations of whole phrases could potentially be reused between related languages. Moreover, the vocabulary overlap and the similarity in word order can be used to improve the word alignments for the resource-poor language by biasing the word alignment process with additional sentence pairs from the resource-rich language. We take advantage of all these opportunities: (1) we improve the word alignments for the resource-poor language, (2) we further augment it with additional translation options, and (3) we take care of potential spelling differences through appropriate transliteration.

Speaker's Bio

Dr. Preslav Nakov is a Research Fellow at the National University of Singapore. He received his PhD in Computer Science from the University of California at Berkeley in 2007. Dr. Nakov's research interestes are in the areas of Web as a corpus, lexical semantics, machine translation, information extraction, and bioinformatics.

Proceedings of Recent Advances in Natural Language Processing, page 1,
Hissar, Bulgaria, 12-14 September 2011.

Discontinuous Constituents: a Problematic Case for Parallel Corpora Annotation and Querying

Marilisa Amoia, Kerstin Kunz, Ekaterina Lapshinova-Koltunski
Department of Applied Linguistics, Saarland University
{m.amoia,k.kunz,e.lapshinova}@mx.uni-saarland.de

Abstract

In this paper, we discuss some linguistic phenomena that pose potential problems for multilevel linguistic annotation of parallel corpora in general and specifically for data encoding with state-of-art multilevel corpus querying tools such as CQP. We describe the strategy we use for integrating the standard hierarchical XML representation used to annotate such phenomena in our aligned bilingual corpus GECCo into a timeline-based format as used in CQP. Thus, our framework supports efficient multilevel representation as well as corpus exploitation and querying of linguistic data of arbitrary complexity.

1 Introduction

Gathering and providing a natural language corpus of good quality requires the definition of data models that mirror the complexity of natural language data from written as well as spoken discourse. In recent years, much work has been done to develop standards for annotations, annotation schemes and coding practice guidelines (c.f. (McKelvie et al., 2001), (Blache et al., 2010)) with the aim of allowing data exchange between different annotations tools and portability of corpora to other platforms as well as the integration of corpora. Yet, relative little attention has been devoted to interfacing annotation schemes with the encoding formats required by corpus query engines.

Although several efficient automatic systems for parallel corpus exploitation have been developed, these systems are generally specialized for the storage and retrieval of a very limited number of annotation levels. For instance, UNITEX (Paumier, 2000) only allows alignment on sentence level, and although EMDROS (Petersen, 2004) is a system for storing and retrieving annotated texts that is very generic and applicable to almost any kind of linguistic annotation, it does not allow alignment.

In fact, very few corpus query tools such as CQP (Christ, 1994), ANNIS2 (Zeldes et al., 2009) or MATE (McKelvie et al., 2001) exist that can handle multilevel annotated corpora. To our knowledge, ANNIS2 is still in the development phase, at the moment of writing, and MATE (McKelvie et al., 2001) does not easily support alignment of parallel corpora.

In this paper, we present our experience with the multilevel query engine CQP developed within the CWB Open Corpus Workbench (Christ, 1994), a collection of open-source tools for managing and querying large text corpora (ranging from 10 million to 2 billion words).

Our focus will be on some problematic issues that have been raised by our attempt to automatically encode our multilevel-annotated bilingual parallel corpus into CQP. The GECCo corpus, which was developed in our research group for the contrastive study of cohesion in English and German combines automatic and manual annotation on different layers of linguistic knowledge ranging from pos-tagging, syntax chunking to semantic information such as linguistic chains and coreference. We noticed that certain annotations were difficult to encode employing state-of-art query tools, namely those representing discontinuous segments.

The paper is structured as follows: Section 2 gives an overview of linguistic phenomena that might lead to discontinuous segments. Section 3 describes the XML-based data format on which multi-layer annotations in the corpus are based. Section 4 deals with the strategy we adopted to encode corpus annotations into CQP and in particular describes the strategy for encoding problematic constituents such as discontinuous segments into a timeline-based data format, as the one used

Proceedings of Recent Advances in Natural Language Processing, pages 2–10,
Hissar, Bulgaria, 12-14 September 2011.

by CQP, so as to allow corpus querying and exploitation. Section 5 concludes with pointers for future research.

2 Differences in Information Distribution between English and German

This section is concerned with differences in information distribution between English and German as these complicate annotation and exploitation of parallel corpora. Here, structural shifts between originals and translations have turned out to be particularly problematic in view of semi-automatic annotation and querying of translational equivalents or extraction for further processing. They cause discontinuity in cases where the translational equivalents are aligned on the basis of semantic criteria[1].

2.1 Contrasts between English and German

General differences between English and German such as case marking and word order (see e.g. (Hawkins, 1986), (Koenig and Gast, 2007), (Steiner, 2001) and (Teich, 2003)) are believed to have implications with respect to the positional options for the integration of information into sentences. For instance, (Doherty, 2004) but also (Teich, 2003) and (Steiner and Teich, 2004) note that the order of information is more flexible in English at the beginning of declarative main clauses where more than one constituent may occur before the verb complex. In contrast, German offers more structuring options after the finite verb (in the Mittelfeld) and an additional option behind the non-finite verb (Nachfeld). This is due to the topological peculiarity of the German verbal bracket. Fabricius-Hansen (1999) highlights the tendency of German to structure experiential meaning more vertically and metaphorically in contrast to a more horizontal and congruent distribution of information in English. She indicates "recursive compounding, repeated nominalization, heavy prenuclear and postnuclear noun phrase modification, and accumulation of adverbial adjuncts" (Fabricius-Hansen, 1999) as grammatical features that enhance hierarchical information packaging. In summary, the differences between English and German described above may provoke the following relevant shifts between originals and translation: Meaning that is expressed inside phrases in German may be expressed by a subordinate or main clause or may appear in a separate sentence in English. Meaning that is expressed in a medium sentence position in German may be shifted to the beginning or end of a sentence or be incorporated in a separate sentence in English. As a consequence of these shifts we assume that meaning may be conveyed in English by a contiguous element at one particular position, while corresponding meaning may be realized in German by separate elements in different syntactic positions. We thus expect a higher number of discontinuous segments in German, both at phrase and at clause level. In the following section of this paper some examples of discontinuous segments will be discussed.

2.2 Some examples for discontinuous segments

We now go on to examine some stretches of text from the GECCo corpus in which discontinuous segments are encoded in case of semantic alignment. In German, discontinous segments at sentence level may be caused by a tendency to encode relevant information in the form of complex appositions in a middle position of the sentence:

(1) a. Dieser Lösung - und das ist für mich das Wunder - haben zum Schluss alle zugestimmt:

b. The miraculous thing for me was that in the end everyone agreed to this solution:

In the German original (1a), relevant and focused information is inserted as a clausal apposition into another sentence, without being related to one specific constituent. The same meaning is expressed in the English translation (1b) by the subject and predicate of the main clause turning the predicate plus arguments of the German main clause in a subordinate clause. The alignment of translational equivalents therefore requires the annotation of a discontinuous segment. Below is an example of a discontinuous segment in German that is not only annotated for alignment of translational equivalents but also for the annotation of coreference.

(2) a. Sehr erfolgreich ist - und das bestätigen mir vor Ort nicht nur sozialdemokratische Kommunalpolitiker - das Förderprogramm InnoRegio.

[1]We opted for a semantic alignment as we assume that only this kind of annotation provides the information necessary for studying English-German contrasts in information distribution and further phenomena of cohesion.

b. The InnoRegio funding programme has been very successful – something local politicians, and not just Social Democrats, have confirmed.

In the German original (2a), a clausal apposition is again inserted into another main clause. However, the anaphoric pronoun *das* in the apposition refers to the whole main clause. Thus, the latter has to be annotated as discontinuous segment in order to mark it as the antecedent of the pronoun. In the English translation (2b), the apposition is retained but appears after the main clause, without splitting it into two linear parts. Thus only one continuous element needs to be segmented in the translation for the annotation and alignment of the antecedent. Another cause of discontinuous segments on sentence level are prepositional phrases which, are again distributed more freely in German than in English.

(3) a. Dieser Konsens ist trotz aller möglichen Vorbehalte ein hohes politisches Gut.

b. Despite all possible reservations, this consensus is a key political asset.

A prepositional phrase functioning as an adverbial occurs after the predicate (in the Mittelfeld) in German (3a) but is moved to the beginning of the sentence in the English translation (3b). Consequently, alignment of the main clause according to semantic criteria would result in a discontinuous segment in German but not in English.

(4) a. Dieser Konsens ist, trotz aller möglichen Vorbehalte, ein hohes politisches Gut, das die Stiftung "Erinnerung, Verantwortung und Zukunft" im Kuratorium unter Leitung von Botschafter Kastrup und durch den Vorstand aus Dr. Jansen, Dr. Bräutigam und Botschafter Primor erhalten muß.

b. Despite all possible reservations, this consensus is a key political asset which the Foundation "Remembrance, Responsibility and the Future" must preserve on its Board of Trustees. The latter is chaired by Ambassador Dieter Kastrup. Board of Trustees members Michael Jansen, Hans-Otto Bräutigam, and Ambassador Avi Primor were elected the foundation's executive officers.

In the German excerpt, a prepositional phrase functioning as an adverbial occurs in the Mittelfeld (4a) before the right verbal bracket. The meaning of this PP is realized in a separate sentence in the English translation (4b). A meaning-based alignment of the first English sentence therefore includes a discontinuous element in the German original.

Discontinuous segments on phrase level in German may be due to distinct NP pre-modification conventions (see (Koenig and Gast, 2007), (Doherty, 2004), (Fabricius-Hansen, 1999) and (Teich, 2003)). In contrast to English, merely prepositional phrases and finite relative clauses follow the head noun in German. Constructions of medium complexity are usually placed before the head noun. These contrasts may complicate coreference chaining, on the one hand, and alignment of elements of these chains in the parallel corpora, on the other hand.

(5) a. über zwei Zeilen Lagerhäuser blicken wir auf [das strömungslose Grau des Hafenbeckens und auf die Landzunge, die sich zwischen ihm und dem Fluss erstreckt]_$A1$. Seit Menschengedenken gehört [dieses auf drei Seiten von Wasser umgebene Gelände]_$B1$ der chemischen Industrie.

b. We look across two rows of warehouses at [the motionless grey surface of the harbor basin and the tongue of land that extends between it and the river]_$A2$. Enclosed on three sides by water, [this area]_$B2$ has been a preserve of the chemical industry for as long as anyone can remember.

The German antecedent (A1) and its English translational equivalent (A2) exhibit similar NP structures. At the same time, there are some positional differences between the German anaphor (B1) and the corresponding anaphor in the English translation (B2): While the German noun phrase contains several premodifying elements, the English anaphor only consists of the demonstrative determiner and the head noun. The reason for this is that the non-finite predicate argument construction "auf drei Seiten von Wasser umgebene" inserted between the demonstrative determiner and the nominal head in German could not be realized as premodifier in English. The translator chose to separate it from the rest of the noun phrase and transformed it into an adverbial clause functioning as a clausal adverbial at sentence level. Hence, semantic alignment of the English subject "this area" results in the annotation of a discontinuous segment in German, consisting of "diese" and "Gelände". Flexible positioning of complex NP postmodifiers in German may also yield discontinuous segments:

(6) a. This occurred just after I took a turning and found myself on a road curving around the edge of a hill.

b. Dies geschah kurz nach einer Abzweigung, als ich mich plötzlich auf einer Straße befand, die in Kurven an einem Hang entlangführte.

The relative clause occurs after the nominal head in both the English original and its German translation. However, the heavy NP shift enables the German relative clause to be postponed after the predicate. The alignment of the corresponding relative clauses entails annotating a discontinuous element in German.

(7) a. Aber wenn die Notwendigkeit von Reformen besser verstanden wird, als die Bereitschaft verbreitet ist, diese zu unterstützen (...)

b. However, if the awareness of necessary reforms is greater than the willingness to support these reforms (...)

In the example above, the infinitive plus argument postmodifying the NP head "Bereitschaft" occurs after the predicate, while the corresponding infinitive construction appears directly after the NP head "willingness" in English. The alignment of both noun phrases requires the creation of a discontinuous segment in German.

Although we assume that the number of discontinuous segments may be higher in the German than in the English corpus, for the reasons highlighted above, note should be made of the fact that English-German contrasts may also trigger discontinuous elements in the English corpus as illustrated by the following example:

(8) a. What is now clear from the historical evidence of the last century is that in every case where a poor nation has significantly overcome its poverty, this has been achieved while engaging in production for export markets and opening itself to the influx of foreign goods, investment and technology; that is, by participating in globalization."

b. Anhand der historischen Beweise des letzten Jahrhunderts ist jetzt klar, da in jedem Fall, in dem eine arme Nation ihre Armut in beträchtlichem Maße überwunden hat, dies durch die Produktion für Exportmärkte und die eigene Öffnung für ausländische Waren, Investitionen und Technologie geschah - das heißt, durch die Beteiligung an der Globalisierung."

Pseudo-cleft constructions as employed in the example above are a rather frequent strategy in English for realizing clauses as subjects in Theme position (see (Teich, 2003)). Equivalent constructions are relatively rare in German, and indeed, the meaning of the English pseudo-cleft clause is realized as a main clause in the German translation. As a consequence, the complex prepositional phrase of the English pseudo-cleft is moved to the beginning of the sentence in German. An alignment of these two PPs therefore entails the creation of other discontinuous segments in the English original.

Other differences between English and German causing discontinuous segments especially in English may result from the greater availability of non-finite verb constructions or a more verbal realization of meaning in general.

3 Annotation of Parallel Corpora

3.1 GECCo: A Multilingual Parallel Corpus

Our multilingual parallel corpus GECCo, which is an extended version of the CroCo corpus (cf. (Neumann, 2005)), was specifically designed to support contrastive studies of English and German texts as described in the above examples. To our knowledge, it represents one of the few existing resources containing annotation of cohesive devices in parallel multilingual corpora. This type of information plays a crucial role not only in contrastive linguistics and translation studies but also in numerous NLP research areas. Most of the information encoded in the corpus was annotated manually. Further, the corpus includes manual clause alignment.

Aligned Clauses

English:

[when they put it back in] $_{cl:53\_EN}$

German:

[wenn sie es wieder einsetzten] $_{cl:40\_GE}$

Word Layer

English:

```
<token id="t310" string="when"/ >
<token id="t311" string="they"/ >
<token id="t312" string="put"/ >
<token id="t313" string="it"/ >
<token id="t314" string="back"/ >
<token id="t315" string="in"/ >
```

German:

```
<token id="t326" string="wenn"/ >
<token id="t327" string="sie"/ >
<token id="t328" string="es"/ >
<token id="t329" string="wieder"/ >
<token id="t330" string="einsetzten"/ >
```

Chunk Layer

English:

```
<chunk id="ch132" type="conj" gf="conj">
  <tok xlink:href="t310"/ >
< /chunk>

<chunk id="ch133" type="np" gf="subj">
   <tok xlink:href="t311"/ >
< /chunk>

<chunk id="ch134" type="vp_fin"
gf="fin">
  <tok xlink:href="t312"/ >
  <tok xlink:href="t315"/ >
< /chunk>

<chunk id="ch135" type="np" gf="dobj">
   <tok xlink:href="t313"/ >
< /chunk>

<chunk id="ch136" type="advp"
gf="adv_loc">
  <tok xlink:href="t314"/ >
< /chunk>
```

German:

```
<chunk id="ch123" type="conj" gf="conj">
  <tok xlink:href="t326"/ >
< /chunk>

<chunk id="ch124" type="np" gf="subj">
  <tok xlink:href="t327"/ >
< /chunk>

<chunk id="ch125" type="np" gf="dobj">
  <tok xlink:href="t328"/ >
< /chunk>

<chunk id="ch126" type="advp"
gf="adv_temp">
   <tok xlink:href="t329"/ >
< /chunk>

<chunk id="ch127" type="vp_fin"
gf="fin">
   <tok xlink:href="t330"/ >
< /chunk>
```

Figure 1: Example of Corpus Annotation Layers in GECCo.

For the time being, GECCo contains 10 different registers, i.e. the eight registers of written language of the CroCo corpus and two new registers (interviews and academic discourse) of spoken language (see (Kunz and Koltunski, 2011) for a more detailed description of the GECCo corpus architecture). We are currently trying to enhance the automatic annotation of the new registers by means of manual annotation. Encoding the different layers of manual annotation into CQP, we are faced with the difficulty of encoding discontinuous constituents as illustrated in section 2.

In conclusion we can say that the complexity of linguistic annotations required for studying contrasts in English-German cohesive devices necessitates both

(i) an annotation scheme capable of coping with multilevel annotations, i.e. graph structures and

(ii) a multilevel corpus query engine that can cope with the complexity of our annotation layers and data model.

3.2 Annotation data model

XML is generally considered to be a useful tool for encoding complex structured language data. Indeed, XML is a widely used standard for encoding annotations of natural language corpora. Although the base formalism cannot describe overlapping structures since it was originally designed to represent tree structures only, its extension (Isard and Thompson, 1998) with hyperlinks (*href*) enables the representation of crossing and overlapping structures.

In our corpus annotation framework we have adopted a modular strategy. Each annotation layer is represented as a different XML file generated by MMAX2 (Müller and Strube, 2006) that supports the manual annotation. The mapping of different representation layers (the graph structure) is guaranteed by the (href) hyperlinks between the different XML files. Figure 1 shows some example annotations from the corpus.

In order to allow further corpus query and exploitation, the linguistic information contained in the XML files needs to be merged into a format readable by a corpus query engine. As this operation is not straightforward in the case of discontinuous segments, an overview of the potential difficulties will be provided in the following section.

.

4 Interfacing XML Annotations of Discontinuous Segments in CQP

4.1 CQP data model

CQP is based on an XML-like corpus encoding language that is compatible with the data model we use for corpus annotation.

The primary data used in CQP are tokens. The CQP language is a rigid positional system on the token positions, i.e. the tokens are totally ordered, providing a timeline for the incremental encoding of structural attributes. CQP provides annotations of two types of attributes:

- positional attributes: describe features related to the tokens or token position such as part-of-speech, morphological features, etc.
- structural attributes: describe features related to ordered sets of tokens, such as syntactic chunks, clauses, sentences, etc.

CQP allows for incremental information merging, i.e. structural attributes can be sequentially integrated with the positional attributes so as to refine the linguistic information present in the corpus. Figure 2 displays an example of incremental annotation encoding in CQP.

Further, CQP enables the representation of overlapping structures, which is not allowed in standard XML. However, as CQP uses the positions of tokens for storage and retrieval, discontinuous segments cannot be directly represented.

In conclusion we can say that, in order to encode the GECCo corpus annotation data into CQP, the hierarchical XML representation used for encoding multi-layer annotations needs to be translated into the CQP timeline-based corpus representation on the basis of the position of tokens. The next section describes the strategy we employ for encoding discontinuous constituents into CQP.

4.2 Representing discontinuous segments in CQP

As we have seen previously, structural attributes are encoded in CQP as ordered sets of token positions. Thus, a structural attribute TAG describing an XML tag (e.g. *token* or *chunk*) can be defined as the following sequence of token positions:

$$TAG = [t_1, t_2, ..., t_n],$$

with $[1, 2, ..., n]$ being a continuous sequence. Therefore, in a TAG attribute no gaps are allowed.

```
Step1: tokens
311: they
312: put
313: it
314: back
315: in

Step 2: morphology
311: they_Pro_plural
312: put _Verb
313: it _Pro_singular
314: back_Adv
315: in_Adv

Step 3: syntax
<np>
311: they_Pro_plural
< /np>
<vp>
312: put _Verb
313: it _Pro_singular
314: back_Adv
315: in_Adv
< /vp>
```

Figure 2: Merging multi-layer XML annotations into CQP.

In order to describe the strategy used to encode discontinuous segments into CQP, we first give the formal definition of a discontinuous structural attribute.

Let TAG be a sequence of tokens describing the structural attribute represented by an XML tag

$$TAG = [t_1, ..., t_j, ..., t_{j+n}, ..., t_k]$$

and $GAPS$ a set of integer pairs such that

$(x_i, y_i) \in GAPS$ iff
$[x_i, x_i{+}1, ..., y_i]$ is a sequence of integer numbers without gaps

Then, the definition of a discontinuous sequence is as follows:

TAG is discontinuous iff
$\mid GAPS \mid > 1$

As CQP does not support the representation of such discontinuous segments we adopt the following strategy: First, we split a TAG containing gaps into the set of its continuous subsets ($\cup TAG_i$), i.e. sequences of tokens without gaps

```
<chunk id="ch133" gf=subj>
  <token id="t311" string="they"/ >
< /chunk>
<chunk id="ch134" gap_id="ch134-gap" gf=fiv>
  <token id="t312" string= "put"/ >
< /chunk>
<chunk id="ch135" gf=dobj>
  <token id="t313" string="it"/ >
< /chunk>
<chunk id="ch136" gf=adv_loc>
   <token id="t314" string="back"/ >
< /chunk>
<chunk id="ch134" gap_id="ch134-gap" gf=fiv>
   <token id="t315" string="in"/ >
< /chunk>
```

Figure 3: CQP XML-like representation of discontinuous segments.

$$TAG = \cup TAG_i, \text{ e.i.}$$
$$= \cup[x_i, ..., y_i], \forall(x_i, y_i) \in GAPS$$

Then, after having assigned an identical coindex *gap_id* to all the subsets of a discontinuous TAG, we represent each of them as a standard CQP structural attribute. At the query stage, the segments that have been split are linked together into a unique segment by a query macro that selects structural attributes with the same *gap_id*.

Summing up, the strategy we adopt consists of three steps:

- partitioning the discontinuous segment into a set of continuous subsets,
- representation of the continuous partitions of the original set as standard CQP structural attributes,
- reconstruction of the original discontinuous segment at the query stage.

An example of a structure that cannot be directly encoded in CQP was given in Figure 1. The English aligned clause contains a discontinuos TAG segment representing a finite verb vp_fin (*put in*).

vp_fin = [t312,t315],
Gap_{vp_fin}=[(312,312),(315,315)]

Figure 3 shows the CQP encoding of the continuous subsets of vp_fin defined by Gap_{vp_fin} for this example.

After segment reconstruction, CQP will extract the expected aligned finite verb chunks from the clause-aligned German/English corpus:

199090: <clause id="GO _SPEECH_009-cl67" align="G2E_SPEECH_009-cl67-cl93">
Dieser Lösung
</clause>
→etrans:<clause id="ETRANS_SPEECH_009-cl93" align="G2E_SPEECH_009-cl67-cl93">
that in the end everyone agreed to this solution
</clause>

199093: <clause id="GO_SPEECH_009-cl68" align="G2E_SPEECH_009-cl68-cl92">
und das ist für mich das Wunder
</clause>
→etrans:<clause id="ETRANS_SPEECH_009-cl92" align="G2E_SPEECH_009-cl68-cl92>
The miraculous thing for me was
</clause>

199101: <clause id="GO_SPEECH_009-cl67" align="G2E_SPEECH_009-cl67-cl93">
haben zum Schluss alle zugestimmt
</clause>
→etrans:<clause id="ETRANS_SPEECH_009-cl93" align="G2E_SPEECH_009-cl67-cl93">
that in the end everyone agreed to this solution
</clause>

Figure 4: CQP representation of alignment in GECCo.

vp_fin_EN = *[put in]*
vp_fin_GE = *[einsetzen]*

Figure 4 represents the output obtained by querying the GECCo corpus with CQP. In particular, it shows how the framework described in this paper permits both an efficient encoding and querying of linguistic annotations (e.g. the alignment of linguistic discontinuous constituents such as (1) with (2)) in CQP.

5 Conclusion

In this paper, we have discussed problematic issues that may arise in connection with the automatic encoding of a manually annotated corpus into the multilevel corpus query engine CQP. Manual corpus annotation often produces complexly structured representations of the linguistic information displayed in the corpus that are difficult to encode using general state-of-art corpus query tools.

While much research has addressed the issue of providing annotation standards for linguistic corpora, only a few resources (e.g. ANNIS2 and MATE) exist that provide efficient interfacing of those multi-layer annotations standards with corpus query engines. However, MATE (McKelvie et al., 2001) does not support parallel corpora encoding. ANNIS 2 (Zeldes et al., 2009) for instance provides translation utilities from arbitrary XML data structures to the ANNIS format. The Annis2 representation format allows the representation and graphs and discontinuous constituents of arbitrary complexity. However, the corpus query language provided by this system is highly complex and requires a high level of expertise on the part of the user.

In this paper we proposed a CQP-based alternative to ANNIS2. We described the strategy we implemented that allows the encoding and querying in CQP of multi-layer parallel corpora that include linguistic phenomena of arbitrary complexity.

Our framework compares well with frameworks such as the one implemented into ANNIS 2 in that it combines all the advantages of the corpus query engine CQP, e.g. efficient querying of very large text corpora, efficient querying of parallel corpora and an intuitive and user-friendly corpus query language, with a framework for encoding arbitrary complex data structures into CQP.

Acknowledgments

The authors thank the DFG (Deutsche Forschungsgemeinschaft) for supporting this project.

References

Philippe Blache, Brigitte Bigi, Laurent Prévot, Stéphane Rauzy, and Julien Seinturier. 2010. A general scheme for broad-coverage multimodal annotation. In *Proceedings of ICGL-10*.

Oli Christ. 1994. A modular and flexible architecture for an integrated corpus query system. In *COMPLEX'94*.

M. Doherty. 2004. Strategy of incremental parsimony. *SPRIKreports*, No 25.

C. Fabricius-Hansen. 1999. Information packaging and translation: Aspects of translational sentence splitting (german/english/norwegian). *Studia Grammatica*, 47:175–214.

J. A. Hawkins. 1986. *A Comparative Typology of English and German: Unifying the Contrasts*. Croom Helm, London.

McKelvie D. Isard, A. and H.S. Thompson. 1998. Dialogue transcripts: A new sgml architecture for the hcrc map task corpus. In *Proceedings of the 5th International Conference on Spoken Language Processing, ICSLP98*, Sydney.

E. Koenig and V. Gast. 2007. *Understanding English-German Contrasts. Grundlagen der Anglistik und Amerikanistik*. Schmidt (revised 2nd edition: 2009), Berlin.

Kerstin Kunz and Ekaterina Lapshinova Koltunski. 2011. Tools to analyse german-english contrasts in cohesion. In *Hamburg Working Papers in Multilingualism*.

David McKelvie, Amy Isard, Andreas Mengel, Morten Baun Mller, Michael Grosse, and Marion Klein. 2001. The mate workbench - an annotation tool for xml coded speech corpora. *Speech Communication*, pages 97–112.

Christoph Müller and Michael Strube. 2006. Multilevel annotation of linguistic data with MMAX2. In Sabine Braun, Kurt Kohn, and Joybrato Mukherjee, editors, *Corpus Technology and Language Pedagogy: New Resources, New Tools, New Methods*, pages 197–214. Peter Lang, Frankfurt a.M., Germany.

S. Neumann. 2005. Corpus design. *Deliverable of the CroCo Project*, No 1.

Sébastien Paumier. 2000. Nouvelles méthodes pour la recherche d'expressions dans de grands corpus. In A. Dister, editor, *Actes des 3èmes Journées INTEX. Revue Informatique et Statistique dans les Sciences Humaines, 36éme annèe, n 1 à 4*.

Ulrik Petersen. 2004. Emdros: a text database engine for analyzed or annotated text. In *COLING '04: Proceedings of the 20th international conference on Computational Linguistics*. Association for Computational Linguistics.

Erich Steiner and Elke Teich. 2004. *Metafunctional profile of the grammar of German.* In: Caffarel, A., J.R. Martin and C.M.I.M. Matthiessen (eds). Language Typology. A Functional Perspective. Benjamins, Amsterdam.

Erich Steiner. 2001. Translations englishgerman: investigating the relative importance of systemic contrasts and of the text type translation. *SPRIKreports*, No 7:1–49.

E. Teich. 2003. *Cross-linguistic variation in system and text. A methodology for the investigation of translations and comparable texts*. De Gruyter, Berlin and New York.

Amir Zeldes, Julia Ritz, Anke Lüdeling, and Christian Chiarcos. 2009. Annis: A search tool for multilayer annotated corpora. In *Proceedings of Corpus Linguistics 2009, Liverpool, July 20-23, 2009.*

A tagged and aligned corpus for the study of Proper Names in translation

Emeline Lecuit
LLL
Université François Rabelais
France
emeline.lecuit@univ-tours.fr

Denis Maurel
LI
Université François Rabelais
France
denis.maurel@univ-tours.fr

Duško Vitas
Faculty of mathematics
University of Belgrade
Serbia
vitas@matf.bg.ac.rs

Abstract

In this paper, we propose the creation of a tagged and aligned corpus for the study of a linguistic phenomenon, the translation of proper names. We try to modify the hypothesis according to which proper names cannot be translated and should therefore appear as borrowings in a target-language. To do so, we introduce a parallel multilingual corpus made of eleven versions in ten different languages of a novel. One of these versions, the French one, which appears to be the source-text, undergoes named entity extraction so as to localize more easily the phenomenon we try to study. We focus on the tools used for the creation of our corpus and present some results refuting the idea that proper names are not translatable.

1 Introduction

The idea according to which proper names cannot be translated seems to be unfortunately widely spread. This can lead to big translation mistakes. Nevertheless it can easily be explained by a long tradition of presenting proper names as belonging to a linguistic category often defined using very reductive criteria which seem to have a very long life ahead of them. We have a different opinion and believe that proper names can be translated and are translated more often than people seem to think. We therefore introduce a multilingual corpus which will help us defend our idea. This corpus is created using several NLP tools, including cascade transducers for the extraction of named entities and an alignment tool, for the alignment of the eleven versions of the same text composing our corpus.

This study is therefore a good example both of the creation of an annotated multilingual corpus and of its usability.

In Section 2 we present the text(s) composing our corpus and the problem we try to tackle, giving details about what a proper name can be. In Section 3 we describe the extraction and annotation of the proper names in the French text of our corpus, using the Named Entity extractor CasEN. In section 4, the different steps for the creation of our multilingual corpus, using the alignment tool XAlign, are presented. Section 5 contains some preliminary answers to our translation problem and a conclusion.

2 A corpus for the observation of a linguistic phenomenon

When talking about translating proper names, a French person could argue: "Je m'appelle Paul et mon nom ne change pas si je me rends à Londres"[1], which is correct. But Paul's plane is going to land in *London*, and not *Londres*.

A lot of people believe that proper names are never translated. This idea, though widely spread and defended by many (from Moore[2] to Kleiber, 1981) can be discussed.

Our hypothesis is that proper names are, just like any other linguistic unit, subject to translation processes of all sorts (from borrowing to adaptation through calque and literal translation, etc.) when transferred from a text in source-language to a text in target-language (as demonstrated by Agafonov *et al.*,

1 "I am called Paul and my name doesn't change if I go to London."

2 See Ballard, 2001

Proceedings of Recent Advances in Natural Language Processing, pages 11–18,
Hissar, Bulgaria, 12-14 September 2011.

2006). To defend our hypothesis we use a parallel multilingual corpus, built with different versions (i.e. in different languages) of the same novel, *Le Tour du Monde en quatre-vingts jours* (*Around the World in eighty days*), written by the famous French author Jules Verne, in 1872. The choice of this novel amongst others was motivated by two main reasons. Firstly, there exist lots of translations of this novel. Indeed, Verne's novel was translated in many languages and is nowadays available on the Internet in almost all European languages. Secondly, there is an important number of proper names of all sorts in this novel. This may be due to the fact that the novel deals with the adventures of Phileas Fogg, a rich and enigmatic English character who, after a bet with his fellows from the Reform-Club, has to go around the world in less than 80 days and who therefore travels through many countries and also happens to meet a lot of people. The novel references proper names belonging to almost all the existing categories and sub-categories of proper names.

Proper names can refer to people (or group of people) real or fictitious (we call these proper names anthroponyms), to places (toponyms), to human productions (ergonyms), or to events (pragmonyms). Though the common idea of a proper name is a simple lexical unit (in the form of a family name, for example), proper names can be complex lexical units, composed of several proper names and/or adjectives, common names, etc. Consider the following examples: *Passepartout* and l'*Institution royale de la Grande-Bretagne* (the *Royal Institution of Great-Britain*), both taken from the novel, though very different in structure, are proper names.

In our corpus, we gather eleven versions of the novel: starting from the original French version. We also have two English versions (by two different translators, at two very different periods and oriented towards two very different audiences[3]), as well as one version in German, one in Spanish, one in Italian, one in Portuguese, one in Serbian (using a Roman alphabet), one in Bulgarian, one in Polish and one in Greek. This variety of languages allows us to observe the phenomenon on languages belonging to different families. Once the different versions of the text gathered, we need to isolate the units we want to study in the French version of our text and to align the different versions to facilitate the study.

3 Annotation of the proper names using CasEN

To have a clearer view of the items we want to study, it seems a good idea to isolate them using a named entity extractor. We decided to use the resource CasEN (Friburger and Maurel, 2004), which uses the tool CasSys, which is now available on the well-known platform Unitex (Paumier, 2006)[4]. The CasSys system applies a series of finite-state transducers to a text. Each transducer describes a local grammar for the recognition of some entities. The result is a text in which the objects to be studied are marked with indicative tags. The transducer cascade can only be applied to texts which have undergone a preprocessing (division of the text into sentences, tagging using dictionaries, etc.). Only after this first stage the series of transducers can be applied (one after the other, in a defined order) to the text and locate the different contexts that can indicate the presence of the object looked for. In our case, the objects looked for are all kinds of proper names. The transducers we use are extracted from a list of transducers created for the French Ester campaign.

The objects we need to extract are basically persons, organizations and places. Once localized, these objects receive the following tags:

pers (*person*)
  pers.hum (*human*), pers.anim (*animal*)
org (*organization*)
  org.pol (*political*), org.edu (*educational*), org.com (*commercial*), org.non-profit (*non commercial*), org.div (*media and recreation*), org.gsp (*administrative*)
loc (*location*)
  loc.geo (*geographical*), loc.admi (*administrative*), loc.line, loc.fac (*facilities*)
  loc.addr (*address*), loc.addr.post, loc.addr.tel, loc.addr.elec

[3] Comparing these two versions will show us if the phenomenon of translation of proper names can be affected when these factors vary.

[4] For more information, see http://tln.li.univ-tours.fr/Tln_CasEN.html. The transducers are available for download from this website.

prod (*product*)
prod.vehicule, prod.award, prod.art, prod.doc

Figure 1 below is an example of transducer.

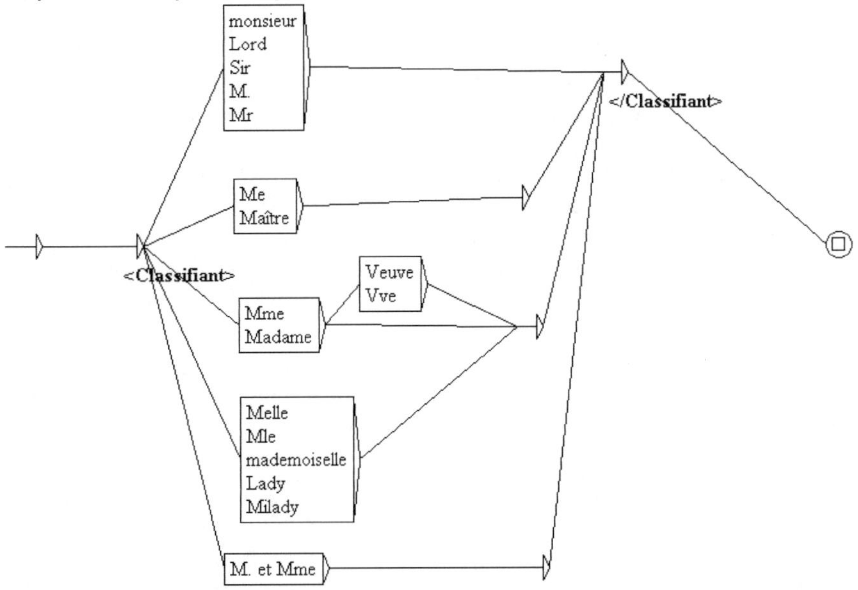

Figure 1: A transducer describing titles introducing person proper names

Let us illustrate the annotation of proper names in our corpus. When we apply the selected transducers (as explained above) to our French text; the input text:

> En l'année 1872, la maison portant le numéro 7 de Saville-row, Burlington Gardens - maison dans laquelle Sheridan mourut en 1814 - , était habitée par Phileas Fogg, esq., l'un des membres les plus singuliers et les plus remarqués du Reform-Club de Londres, bien qu'il semblât prendre à tâche de ne rien faire qui pût attirer l'attention.

becomes the tagged text:

> En l'année 1872, la maison portant le numéro 7 de **<ENT type="loc.line">**Saville-row **</ENT>**, **<ENT type="loc.line">** Burlington Gardens**</ENT>** -- maison dans laquelle **<ENT type="pers.hum">** Sheridan**</ENT>** mourut en 1814 --, était habitée par **<ENT type="pers.hum">**Phileas Fogg, esq. **</ENT>**, l'un des membres les plus singuliers et les plus remarqués du **<ENT type="org.div">**Reform-Club de Londres **</ENT>**, bien qu'il semblât prendre à tâche de ne rien faire qui pût attirer l'attention.

where each recognized proper name receives a tag indicating its category and sub-category.

After applying the cascade, a checking was carried out and some corrections were manually made (some tags were expanded or reduced, i.e. the brackets were moved to adjust to the entity, and others were deleted, added, or modified).

This first phase of our work provides us with a tagged text, in which all the proper names can be easily located using simple requests.

Our French version of the text comprises 3415 proper names (519 different). These proper names represent 8.6% of all the characters in the text and 8% of all the words in the text[5].

The following stage consists in aligning all the different versions of our text with the French one and all together.

5 According to Coates-Stephens (1993), this figure can reach 10% in newspaper articles, which shows the importance of these units in texts and explains our involvement in this subject.

4 Alignement of the texts using XAlign

XAlign is a text aligner developed by the LORIA (2006) and available on the Unitex Platform. It combines the performances of an alignment tool to those of a well-know corpus processing system. One of the advantages offered by XAlign is the possibility to reuse an alignment already existing. This NLP tool allows the treatment of two texts at a time, which means that to obtain our multilingual corpus, we first have to align the texts two by two. In fact, we align the French text with all the other versions individually.

Prior to the alignment each translation is transformed into a TEI format and marked at a sentence, paragraph and division level with respectively <s>, <p> and <div> tags. Id attributes are also added to the texts. All these markers will function as explicit anchor points which will help the alignment of the texts. Other potential anchor points, such as proper names, for example will also help the alignment. The alignment will extract the complete optimum path (following a pre-defined set of transitions, 1:1 equivalence, 1:2 equivalence, 2:1 equivalence, etc.). This alignment is represented as a double window, with one version of the text (in one language) on the left side and the other version of the text (in another language) on the right side. Between these two versions, red lines link the translation equivalents. The alignment is therefore visual and easy to consult (see Paumier and Dimitriu, 2008). Below is an example of alignment.

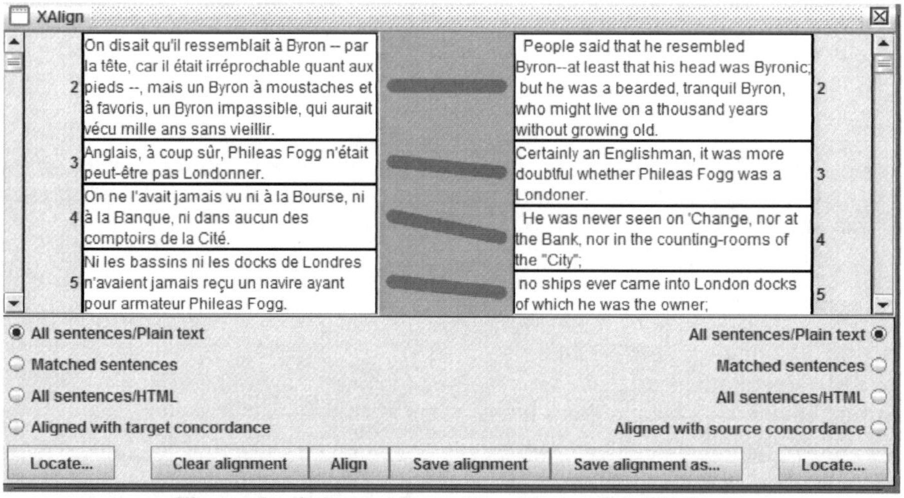

Figure 2 : Extract of an alignment using XAlign

This alignment will be saved as an alignment file in the XAlign directory in Unitex. The alignment file, in XML format, lists all the "linkings" and "alignments" between the two texts. The linkings correspond to links between two (or more) segments of one of the two versions, when the alignments are of type 1:2 or 2:1, for example, meaning that two segments in one version correspond to one segment in the other version or vice versa. The linking indicated in the alignment file (see Figure 3) means that the two segments will be considered as a whole.

<link targets="\\Private \Unitex2.0\French\Corpus\vern-fr-01-37-fixed.xml#d2p8s6 \\Private\Unitex2.0\French\Corpus\vern-fr-01-37-fixed.xml#d2p8s7" **type="linking" xml:id="l1"** />

Figure 3 : XAlign Alignment file (linking)

The alignments indicate, using the id codes applied during the preprocessing, equivalent segments in the first and second texts (see Figure 4).

```
<link
targets="\\Private\Unitex2.0\French\Corpus\vern-fr-01-37-fixed.xml#d6p20s1 \\Private\Unitex2.0\English\Corpus\vern-En-01-37-fixed.xml#d6p20s1" type="alignment" />
```

Figure 4: XAlign alignment file (alignment)

One of the advantages offered by XAlign is that, because it is hosted by Unitex, it is quite easy to do requests on the texts, thanks to the option "XAlign Locate Pattern". Another advantage is that the alignment can easily be modified/corrected.

Now that we have created all our bitexts (alignments of the French text with the other versions individually), proofread and corrected them when needed, we can gather all the bitexts in one big multitext (alignment of all the texts). This is easily done manually. We obtain a big table, allowing us to visualize all the equivalent segments of our texts in the different languages. The table in Annexe is an extract of our Multilanguage corpus (It shows the first sentence of the text aligned in the different versions, with the French tagged version on the left side).

This tagged and aligned corpus allows us to carry on our study of proper names in translation.

5 Results and conclusion

We have created a tagged and aligned corpus for the study of a linguistic phenomenon. Tagged corpora and aligned corpora exist. What makes our corpus interesting is the high number of languages represented and the nature of the text used. Indeed, most multilingual corpora are made of versions of law texts (see for example multilingual corpora of the European Union law texts). Vaxelaire (2006) explains that choice of non-literary texts for the study of proper names because in literary texts "tous les types de noms propres peuvent être modifiés [...]ou changés par des noms qui ne peuvent être considérés comme des équivalents que dans ce contexte précis[..].", which can be translated as follows : " all the types of proper names can be modified [...] or changed into names which cannot be considered as equivalents except on this special occasion".We propose to study a novel. We will therefore study proper names translated by their equivalents but will also meet the case when a proper name is translated with names which cannot be considered as equivalents of translation. The novel we chose is a bit dated but this makes it available and free of use. Moreover, our corpus is extendable. Indeed, there are lots of other versions of the text not considered here which could easily be added to our corpus. We have already mentioned that our corpus is ideal for the study of proper names, since there are many of them in the text and of very various types, as can be observed in the table below (see Figure 5).

hypertypes	total number of occurrences	number of different occurrences
anthroponyms	2079	162
toponyms	1142	320
ergonyms	186	31
pragmonyms	8	6

Figure 5 : The proper names in the original version

Our study is still in progress. We only present here figures concerning 10% of the proper names of each of the types presented above, i.e. 16 anthroponyms, 32 toponyms, 3 ergonyms and 1 pragmonym. These samples are made of the most used items in each category. These 52 proper names represent 2029 occurrences in the French version, i.e. about 60% of all the proper names in the text.

Figure 6 is a table containing the results for these occurrences.

Target language	Borrowing	assimilation	Partial or total calque	Absence of translation	Other processes
English (1st version)	69,1%	11,3%	2,2%	12,1%	5,4%
English (2nd version)	74,2%	13,2%	2,0%	6,6%	4,1%
German	79,7%	10,6%	3,7%	5,2%	0,6%
Polish	31,1%	53,4%	4,5%	10,7%	0,2%
Serbian (Latin alphabet)	4,9%	89,1%	4,5%	0,3%	1,3%
Bulgarian	0,0%	90,6%	6,3%	2,5%	0,7%
Greek	0,0%	86,8%	4,6%	3,5%	5,1%
Italian	72,0%	21,5%	2,6%	3,0%	1,0%
Portuguese	73,7%	16,0%	5,9%	4,1%	0,2%
Spanish	51,6%	15,5%	25,1%	7,4%	0,4%

Figure 6: Translation processes (results)

What we can conclude from the study of these linguistic units is that the wide-spread hypothesis according to which proper names cannot be translated can be discussed.

Indeed, it appears that according to their type (fictitious or real proper names), according to their category (anthroponyms, toponyms, ergonyms, etc.), according to their use (as simple references, or as metaphors for example), according to their construction (simple or complex units), according to the target-language (sometimes implying different morphologic behaviors, sometimes using different alphabets, etc.), proper names can undergo a variety of translation processes. These phenomena are easily observable thanks to our corpus. Indeed, we can use the French tagged part of our corpus to identify a segment of the text containing a proper name. Then, on the same line of our table, we can visualize the translations of this proper name in the various different languages and analyse them.

If most proper names are simple borrowings from the source-text, as can be seen in Figure 6, many are subject to various assimilation (graphic and/or phonetic), as illustrated in the following example (for complete details about translation processes, see Vinay and Darbelnet, 2004).

FRA	ENG2	SPA	ITA
{ENT type'"pers.hum"}Mrs. **Aouda**{/ENT}, ne voulant pas être vue, se rejeta en arrière.	Not wishing to be seen, Mrs **Aouda** jumped back.	Mistress **Aouida**, no queriendo ser vista, se echó para atrás.	Mrs **Auda**, non volendo esser visita, si ritrasse indietro.

Figure 7 : Borrowings with graphic and/or phonetic assimilation

Our corpus also highlights the transcription processes (also accounted for in the "assimilation" column of Figure 6), which are not surprising in Bulgarian and Greek, both languages using a non Latin alphabet, but more striking in our Serbian (using a Latin alphabet) version. In this version, *Passepartout*, the name of the hero's manservant becomes *Paspartu*, for instance. Partial or total calques mentioned in Figure 6 (see Figure 8 for an example), mainly concern proper names which Jonasson (1994) described as "mixed" and "descriptive-based"[6] proper names, i.e. composed of "pure" proper names and/or other lexical elements, such as adjectives, common names, etc. The absences of translation, especially in the first English version and in

[6] "Mixtes" or " à base descriptives" in the original version.

the Polish version, mainly concern anthroponyms, which are replaced either by pronouns or defined descriptions.

The "other processes" are various: transpositions, free translations, to name just a few. The examples below (Figure 9, Figure 10) illustrate some of these translation techniques.

FRA	ENG	GREK	POR	POL	SPA
Vous allez à {ENT type"'loc.admi"}New York{/ENT}?	Are you going to New York?'	Πηγαίνετε στη Νέα Υόρκη;	Vai para Nova York?	- Jedzie pan do Nowego Jorku?	¿Vais a Nueva York?

Figure 8: Partial Calques from the English *New York* (except for the French, borrowing)

FRA	ENG	POL
Je suis un agent de la {ENT type"'org.com"}Compagnie péninsulaire{/ENT}. Litterally, the Peninsular Company	I work for P. and O.' For Peninsular and Oriental	- Jestem agentem Towarzystwa Morskiego Indii Wschodnich. Literally, the Society Maritime of Oriental India

Figure 9: Free translation (also called adaptation)

FRA	ENG	BUL	GER	POL	SRP
Canal de Suez	Suez Canal	Суецкия канал	Suez-Canal	Kanał Sueski (Sueski is an adjective)	Suecki kanal

Figure 10: Transposition (same semantic content but different syntactic structure)

All these examples, which are just a few of all the examples localized thanks to our corpus, seem to prove that it is wrong to promote the systematic use of borrowings when translating proper names.

References

Agafonov, Claire, Grass, Thierry, Maurel, Denis, Rossi-Gensane, Nathalie. and Agata Savary 2006. " La traduction multilingue des noms propres dans PROLEX ". *Méta*, vol.51, n°4, p.622-636.

Ballard, Michel 2001. *Le Nom propre en traduction*. Paris : Ophrys.

Coates-Stephens, Stephen 1993. " The analysis and acquisition of proper names for the understanding of free text ", in Computers and the Humanities, vol.26, p.441-456.

Friburger, Nathalie and Denis Maurel 2004. "Finite-state transducer cascades to extract named entities in texts", *Theoretical Computer Science*, vol.313, p.94-104.

Jonasson, Kerstin 1994. *Le nom propre: constructions et interpretations*. Louvain-la-Neuve : Duculot.

leiber, Georges 1981. *Problèmes de référence : descriptions définies et noms propres*. Paris : Klincksieck.

LORIA 2006. XAlign (Alignement multilingue). http://led.loria.fr/outils/ALIGN/align.html

Paumier S.ébastie,n 2006. *Unitex 2.0 User Manual*, http://igm.univ-mlv.fr/~unitex~/

Paumier Sébastien and Dumitriu Dana-Marina 2008. "Editable text alignments and powerful linguistic queries", in *Proceedings of the 27th Conference on Lexis and Grammar*, L'Aquila.

Vinay Jean-Paul and Darbelnet Jean 2004. "A Methodology for Translation", in *The Translation Studies Reader*. Venuti L. (eds) : Routledge.

Vitas, Duško, Koeva, Svetla, Krstev, Cvetana and Ivan Obradovic. 2008. "*Tour du monde* through the dictionaries", in *Proceedings of the 27th Conference on Lexis and Grammar*, L'Aquila.

FRA-NP	BUL	ENG1	GER	GREK	POL	POR	SPA	ENG2	ITA
En l'année 1872, la maison portant le numéro 7 de {ENT type'"loc.line"}Saville-row{/ENT}, {ENT type'"loc.line"}Burlington Gardens{/ENT} -- maison dans laquelle {ENT type'"pers.hum"}Sheridan{/ENT} mourut en 1814 -, était habitée par {ENT type'"pers.hum"}Phileas Fogg, esq.{/ENT}, l'un des membres les plus singuliers et les plus remarqués du {ENT type'"org"}Reform-Club de Londres{/ENT}, bien qu'il semblât prendre à tâche de ne rien faire qui pût attirer l'attention.	През 1872 година в къщата на "Савил роу" № 7, Бърлингтън Гардънс – същата, в която през 1814 година почина Шеридан, – сега живееше Филиас Фог. ой беше един от най-странните и видни членове на Реформаторския лондонски клуб, въпреки че сякаш се стараеше да не привлича с нищо вниманието на другите.	Mr. Phileas Fogg lived, in 1872, at No. 7, Saville Row, Burlington Gardens, the house in which Sheridan died in 1814.He was one of the most noticeable members of the Reform Club, though he seemed always to avoid attracting attention;	Im Jahre 1872 wohnte in dem Hause Nummer 7, Saville-Row, Burlington Gardens, - worin Sheridan im Jahre 1814 starb, -- Phileas Fogg, Sq., eines der ausgezeichnetsten und hervorragendsten Mitglieder des Reformclubs zu London, der jedoch dem Anschein nach beflissen war nichts zu thun, was Aufsehen erregen konnte.	Το έτος 1872, στο σπίτι με τον αριθμό 7 της Σαβίλ-ρόου, στην περιοχή Μπέρλινγκτον Γκάρντενς -σπίτι στο οποίο πέθανε ο Σέρι-νταν το 1814- κατοικούσε ο αξιότιμος κύριος Φιλέας Φογκ. Ο κύριος αυτός ήταν ένα από τα πλέον ιδιόρρυθμα και επίλεκτα μέλη της Λέσχης της Μεταρρύθμισης του Λονδίνου, παρ' ότι φαινόταν πως προσπαθούσε να μην κάνει τίποτα που θα μπορούσε να κινήσει την προσοχή των άλλων.	"W roku 1872 dom opatrzony numerem siódmym przy Saville Row w Burlington Gardens - dom, w którym w 1814 zmarł Sheridan * - zamieszkiwał szanowny pan Fileas Fogg, jeden z najwybitniejszych i najbardziej oryginalnych członków klubu "Reforma" w Londynie, choć ze swej strony zdawał się czynić wszystko, by nie zwracać na siebie uwagi.	Em 1872, a casa de número 7 da Saville Row, Burlington Gardens - casa em que Sheridan morrera em 1814 - era habitada por Phileas Fogg, esquire, um dos membros mais singulares e destacados do Reform Club de Londres, apesar de todo seu esforço em evitar, segundo parecia, chamar a atenção sobre si.	En el año 1872, la casa número 7 de Saville-Row, Burlington Gardens -- donde murió Sheridan en 1814- estaba habitada por Phileas Fogg, quien a pesar de que parecia haber tomado el partido de no hacer nada que pudiese llamar la atención, era uno de los miembros más notables y singulares del ReformClub de Londres.	IN the year 1872, No. 7 Savile Row, Burlington Gardens - the house where Sheridan died in 1814 - was occupied by Phileas Fogg, Esq. This gentleman was one of the most remarkable, and indeed most remarked upon, members of the Reform Club, although he seemed to go out of his way to do nothing that might attract any attention.	Nell'anno 1872 la casa numero sette di Saville Row, Bullington Gardens (la casa in cui morì Sheridan nel 1816), era abitata da Phileas Fogg, Esq., che sebbene sembrasse aver giurato di non far nulla che potesse dar nell'occhio, era uno dei più eccentrici e più noti soci del Reform Club di Londra.

Annexe : Extract of the multitext corpus

Building the multilingual TUT parallel treebank

Manuela Sanguinetti
Università di Torino
manuela.sanguinetti@studenti.unito.it

Cristina Bosco
Dipartimento di Informatica,
Università di Torino
bosco@di.unito.it

Abstract

The paper introduces an ongoing project for the development of a parallel treebank for Italian, English and French annotated in the pure dependency format of the Turin University Treebank, i.e. Parallel–TUT. We hypothesize that the major features of this annotation format can be of some help in addressing the typical issues related to parallel corpora, e.g. alignment at various levels. Therefore, benefitting from the tools previously used for TUT, we applied the TUT format to a multilingual sample set of sentences from the JRC-Acquis Multilingual Parallel Corpus and the whole text of the Universal Declaration of Human Rights.

1 Introduction

Parallel corpora are currently considered among the crucial resources both for a variety of NLP tasks, e.g. machine translation and cross-lingual information extraction, and for research in the field of translation studies and contrastive linguistics with respect to terminology and syntax in particular.

Since the utility of parallel corpora is increased by forms of annotation which make explicit the linguistic knowledge involved in the raw data, parallel treebanks have proved to be valuable resources for a number of purposes (see e.g. (Ahrenberg et al., 2010; Grimes et al., 2010; Rios et al., 2009)). As far as translation studies are concerned, the FuSe project (Cyrus, 2006), for example, aims at studying translation shifts in an English-German corpus annotated with regard to the predicate-argument structure, while the LinEs parallel treebank for Swedish and English (Ahrenberg, 2007) focuses on this aspect by means of complete alignments of segment pairs. As for contributes to the improvement of machine translation quality (both rule-based and statistical), a few examples are provided by SMULTRON (Volk et al., 2010), with a constituency-based parallel treebank for English, German and Swedish; the Prague Czech-English Dependecy Treebank (Čmejrek et al., 2004); the Copenhagen Dependency Treebank[1] for Danish, English, German, Italian and Spanish; and the Swedish-Turkish Parallel Treebank (Megyesi et al., 2008).

In this paper, we introduce a new parallel treebank for Italian, English and French, henceforth Parallel–TUT. The annotation schema for this new resource is that of the Turin University Treebank (TUT), which has been applied in a dependency-based treebank used for training of parsing systems and as reference for the evaluation campaigns for Italian parsing. By featuring a rich set of grammatical relations, it shows a representation centered on the predicate-argument structure, a linguistic knowledge that is proximate to semantics and underlies syntax and morphology, essential for the efficient processing of human language. We developed our project also in order to test the hypothesis that this kind of knowledge, and thus the schema representing it, can be useful also in bridging the differences among languages, e.g. in translation.

Therefore, as far as the annotation of the Parallel–TUT corpus is concerned, our approach consists in extending and applying the same tools designed for Italian, within the TUT project, to two other languages, i.e. English and French. The result is the extension of the same format and relations for all the languages of the new parallel corpora, with the same granularity in the representation of the linguistic knowledge. On the one hand, this is motivated by the fact that, as suggested in (Paulussen and Macken, 2010), the use of

[1] http://code.google.com/p/copenhagen-dependency-treebank/

Proceedings of Recent Advances in Natural Language Processing, pages 19–28,
Hissar, Bulgaria, 12-14 September 2011.

different annotating tools and formats for each monolingual corpus may have a negative impact on the following exploitation and processing of corpora, such as alignment at various levels. On the other hand, the literature shows several examples of application to different languages of formats originally developed for a given language, by using the same features of the native format to address new linguistic phenomena encountered in the other languages. For instance, the format of the Prague Dependency Treebank (PDT), developed for Czech, has been afterwards applied to Arabic (Hajič and Zemánek, 2003), or the Penn Treebank format, which has been applied e.g. to Chinese[2] and Arabic[3]. An especially relevant side effect of the application of such kind of methodology consists in increasing the portability across languages of NLP tools and in making available data useful for the comparison and study of models and strategies underlying NLP tools when applied to different languages.
The work presented here aims at going beyond the creation of a parallel treebank where Italian language is included. It aims, in fact, at extending and applying a single treebank schema to other languages, and study how the schema can be meaningfully used to address issues typically related to parallel corpora, e.g. alignment at various levels. The focus of this work is therefore the format of the treebank and the consequence of the application of this format on a parallel corpus.

The remainder of the paper is structured as follows. The next section describes the TUT annotation schema while Section 3 shows the content and size of the corpus on which the schema has been applied. Section 4 describes the annotation process for the three monolingual corpora, while Section 5 shows the alignment issues related to the effects of applying the TUT format to English and French. Finally, we discuss the current state of the project, analyze the future developments of Parallel–TUT and briefly summarize the project.

2 The Turin University Treebank: the resource and its annotation schema

TUT is a resource developed in the last ten years by the Natural Language Processing group of the University of Turin (`http://www.di.unito.it/~tutreeb/`). It currently consists in more than 102,000 annotated tokens (around 3,500 sentences).

The treebank annotation is automatically performed by the Turin University Linguistic Environment (henceforth TULE[4]) (Lesmo et al., 2002; Lesmo, 2007; Lesmo, 2009) and then semi-automatically checked in order to recover errors in the morphological and syntactic annotation. TULE is a rule-based dependency parsing system which includes also the modules needed for tokenization, PoS tagging and morphological analysis, as well as parsing. The parsing module produces a projective dependency tree for each given sentence in input. In the last evaluation campaign for Italian parsing, held in 2009 (Bosco et al., 2009b), TULE achieved the best scores currently at the state of the art (Labelled Attachment Score 88.73), which are very close to the scores known for English parsing.
The core of the treebank is a dependency-based annotation scheme (on which we will focus in this paper), but the resource has been also enriched by the converted versions of all the annotated data in a Penn-like format (Bosco, 2007), in a Combinatory Categorial Grammar format (Bos et al., 2009)[5] and in other constituency-based annotations. This results both in an increased quality of the annotated material and portability of the resource. Beyond allowing the training of parsing systems, TUT has been used as a testbed for evaluation campaigns (Bosco et al., 2007; Bosco et al., 2009a; Bosco et al., 2009b) and analyses of parsing models' performance with respect to variation in tag sets, paradigms and annotation schemes (Bosco and Lavelli, 2010).
As far as the native annotation schema is concerned, a typical TUT tree shows a pure dependency format centered upon the notion of argument structure and applies the major principles of the *Word Grammar* theoretical framework (Hudson, 1984). This is mirrored, for instance, in the annotation of Determiners and Prepositions, which are represented in TUT trees as complementizers of Nouns or Verbs. For instance, in figure 1 the tree for the sentence NEWS-355 from TUT, i.e. *"L'accordo si è spezzato per tre motivi principali"* (The agreement has been broken for three main reasons)[6], shows the features of the an-

[2]See `http://www.cis.upenn.edu/~chinese/`
[3]See `http://www.ircs.upenn.edu/arabic/`

[4]`http://www.tule.di.unito.it/`
[5]`http://www.di.unito.it/~tutreeb/CCG-TUT/`
[6]English translations of the Italian examples are literal

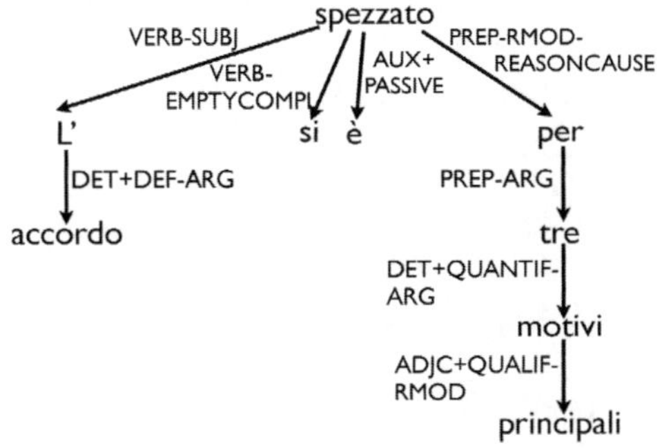

Figure 1: Sentence NEWS–355 of TUT.

notation schema. In particular, we see the role of complementizer played by Determiners (i.e. the article *"L'"* (The) and the numeral *"tre"* (three)) and Prepositions (i.e. *"per* (for)).

By contrast, the native TUT scheme exploits also some representational tools which are non–standard in dependency-based annotations, i.e. null elements, in order to deal with particular structures. In particular, null elements are used for pro–drops and missing subject (e.g. equi), long distance dependencies and elliptical structures. These phenomena are quite common in Italian, a morphologically rich language where verbal inflection leads to a widespread diffusion of the pro–drop phenomenon and to a relatively free order of words and constituents. For instance, the subject deletion is very common with tensed verbs in declarative clauses, as confirmed by the data in TUT corpora, where this phenomenon occurs an average of 0.28 times per sentence[7].

On the one hand, an advantage in using null elements in the annotation is that they permit dependency trees to be without crossing edges and projective structures also for non–projective sentences. On the other hand, by using null elements it is possible to give an explicit representation also of parts of the argument structure that can be missing, but crucial for some task. For instance, in machine translation, if the source language allows argument deletion and the target language does not, in order to make possible for the system to handle the translation, it is crucial that in the source language the dropped argument is explicitly marked. An alike situation can happen in a translation from Italian to English or French, where, on the contrary, the subject is always lexically realized in tensed clauses.

For what concerns the dependency relations that label the tree edges, TUT exploits a rich set of grammatical items designed to represent a variety of linguistic information according to three different perspectives, i.e. morphology, functional syntax and semantics. The main idea is that a single layer, the one describing the relations between words, can represent linguistic knowledge that is proximate to semantics and underlies syntax and morphology, i.e. the predicate-argument structure of events and states, which has proven essential for efficient processing of human language. Therefore, each relation label can in principle include three components, i.e. morpho-syntactic, functional-syntactic and syntactic-semantic, but can be made more or less specialized, including from only one (i.e. the functional-syntactic) to three of them (see e.g. (Bosco and Lavelli, 2010) for more details). For instance, the relation used for the annotation of the Prepositional modifiers in figure 1, i.e. PREP-RMOD-REASONCAUSE (which includes all the three components), can be reduced to PREP-RMOD (which includes only the first two components) or to RMOD (which includes only the functional-syntactic component). This variable degree of specificity is a useful means for the human annotator in that it meets his/her different degree of confidence about a given relation. Moreover, it can also be applied in particular tasks in order to increase the comparability of TUT with other existing resources, by exploiting the amount of linguistic information more adequate for the comparison, e.g. in terms of number of relations.

Last but not least, as Italian requires, the TUT format provides an extended morphological tag set including all the categories and features needed to describe morphologically rich languages. This tag set allowed therefore for an accurate description both for French, whose morphological richness resembles that of Italian, and English, which is morphologically poorer.

Observing related works, we think that the TUT schema can be a good candidate for the development of a parallel treebank for various reasons. First of all, it is oriented to the representation of the predicate-argument structure, a kind of information that can be useful as a pivot for

and s, they thus may appear awkward in English.

[7]But the frequency of pro–drop varies from 0.17 to 0.64 times per sentence according to the text genre included in the treebank.

the alignment in translation, but is also crucial in tasks such as Information Extraction. As observed above, both the dependency core and the inventory of null elements introduced in the annotation schema of TUT contribute to a more accurate representation under this respect. Second, this schema gives the means for the development of annotations at various degrees of specificity of grammatical relations, thus extending the comparability and compatibility with other existing resources. Finally, another aspect to be taken into account is the availability of automatic tools for the conversion of the native TUT format in other constituency-based representations, among which the most known and used format in the world (i.e. that of the Penn Treebank), and in a Combinatory Categorial Grammar format too, which is a semantic-oriented representation.
In the next sections we describe the parallel corpus on which we have applied the TUT format for the development of the Parallel-TUT.

3 The data in the Parallel–TUT

The Parallel–TUT currently comprises a small set of sample texts, which have been annotated in order to assess our methodology and test our hypothesis. They are organized in two sub-corpora, as outlined in Table 1.

The first sub-corpus consists of about 50 sentences extracted from the JRC-Acquis multilingual parallel corpus[8] (Steinberger et al., 2006) for each of the three languages involved in the Parallel–TUT. In particular, the sentences for Italian are shared by TUT and the corpus used within the French parsing evaluation campaign Passage[9], respectively in Italian version annotated in the TUT format, and in French version annotated in the EASy format. The English counterpart of the corpus was retrieved from English section of the JRC-Acquis corpus. We will refer to these data as JRCAcquis–ITA, JRCAcquis–FR and JRCAcquis–EN, respectively for Italian, French and English.
The second sub-corpus, which will be referred as UDHR–ITA, UDHR–FR and UDHR–EN, includes the entire text of the Universal Declaration of Human Rights, as available in the official Web page of the UN Office of the High Commissioner of Human Rights[10], and consists of about 76 sentences for each language.

Corpus	**sentences**	**tokens**
JRCAcquis–ITA	50	2,205
JRCAcquis–FR	52	2,297
JRCAcquis–EN	50	1,895
UDHR–ITA	76	2,387
UDHR–FR	77	2,537
UDHR–EN	77	2,293
total	382	13,614

Table 1: Corpus overview.

For what concerns the texts of the JRCAcquis corpus in particular, they were selected because of their availability in two different annotation formats developed by two independent research groups, as mentioned above. Moreover, choosing texts from legal documents, we benefitted from the expertise in the field of legal language processing acquired within the TUT project[11]. Last but not least, the data included in our corpus are representative of the development of raw text parallel corpora developed in the last decades, e.g. from the European Community. Nevertheless, we know that analyses based on such kind of unbalanced material may lead to misleading results if applied in general context, as the syntax in this corpus is typical of a quite particular kind of documents. This will be taken into account in the further development of our corpus.
In general, our selection of texts includes raw materials which are in translation relation to each other, and free of Intellectual Property Rights problems, which allows us to release treebank data under an open license.

4 Treebank Development

Except for the Italian part of the first sub-corpus of the Parallel–TUT, i.e. JRCAcquis–ITA (which was already available in the annotated version[12] as described above), for the English and French counterparts, as well as for the entire second

[8] See `http://langtech.jrc.it/JRC-Acquis.html`, `http://optima.jrc.it/Acquis/`

[9] `http://atoll.inria.fr/passage/index.en.html`.

[10] See `http://www.ohchr.org/EN/UDHR/Pages/SearchByLang.aspx`

[11] Around the 30% of TUT data are extracted from legal texts, i.e. the *Codice Civile* and the *Costituzione Italiana*.

[12] Available from the TUT Web page at `http://www.di.unito.it/~tutreeb/` (EUDIR Section)

sub-corpus (UDHR), we processed the texts following the same strategies applied in the TUT project and using the same tools both for parsing and checking.
Being the original materials in XML format (eg. texts collected in the JRC multilingual corpus) or directly exctracted from a Web page, the first step was to clean up files from noisy data (eg. markups) and to convert them to plain text files with UTF-8 encoding. In this way, texts can be exploited for our further linguistic analyses.
Despite other parallel treebanks, where monolingual corpora were processed independently with different tools (cf. (Megyesi et al., 2008)), or created from already existing monolingual treebanks (cf.(Klyueva and Mareček, 2010)), the texts of our collection were analyzed from scratch with the same tool, i.e. TULE. Although TULE supports in principle linguistic analysis in several languages (English in particular, but also French, Spanish, Catalan and Hindi), its output quality achieves satisfactory results mostly for Italian, since it has been extensively tested in the development of the Italian treebank TUT. Since TULE is a rule-based parser, the annotation phase for English and French therefore entailed alternating steps of rules insertion in TULE and automatic analysis, until an acceptable output was produced. Rule-insertion steps included mainly the enrichment of lexical knowledge, e.g. insertion of new lexical entries (including proper nouns, named entities, compounds and locutions), modifications in the suffix tables, and new disambiguation rules for linguistic phenomena previously unseen in Italian. A typical example of such phenomena is the English genitive for regular plural nouns (*-s'*). Since in Italian (and French too) the apostrophe is normally considered a graphic sign indicating an elision, during the automatic analysis, tokenization in particular, it is kept attached to the previous token. The English possessive case, however, is normally isolated and treated as a single token. Its recognition in this form by the TULE tokenizer has therefore requested the integration of a new condition in the set of disambiguation rules. Other types of intervention focused on the syntactic representation of those phenomena that distinguish the two languages from Italian. For example, the French superlatives formed by the definite article and *plus/moins* follow a word order which is quite different from that of the Italian superlatives: it was therefore necessary to modify the representation scheme already present in the TUT annotation guidelines for Italian. The treatment of the expletive subject (ie. a purely syntactic subject, not semantically realized), which is a common occurrence both in English and French, but not in Italian (where, as we said, the subject can be omitted) also required the inclusion of additional labels in the annotation schema.
The whole procedure above described had a twofold goal: to improve the output quality of TULE for English and French, and, as a result, to reduce to a feasible extent manual intervention of human annotators in future annotation work.
Because of the current small size of the corpus and the consequently limited training on English and French of our tools, we expect that a considerable amount of manual intervention (eg. enriching the knowledge base of the parsing system) will be necessary also in the next step of the development of our parallel treebank. In fact, the variety of new syntactic structures encountered so far in English and French data is quite small, and the probability that the treebank could miss some syntactic phenomena is high.

The relatively lower quality of the output of TULE for English and French with respect to Italian (as reported in Section 6) made the final stage of manual correction crucial to verify that linguistic phenomena were annotated appropriately and consistently. In this stage, the same tools used in the development of TUT were exploited. For instance, for displaying the dependency trees, the viewerTULETUT Java graphical interface was used, thus allowing the observation of the structures in a more readable graphic form.

It is known that the conversion of dependency trees into phrase structures is in itself a comparative test of the adequateness of the involved representation formats with reference to the features of the language and the quality and consistency of annotation (Musillo and Sima'an, 2002). Therefore, some preliminary experiment was also performed by applying to the English and French data the procedures for the conversion in the Penn Treebank format developed for Italian. The results are promising in particular for English, as we expected, since this is the reference language for the

Penn format. For French the conversion should be further refined by including in the Penn format the representation of particular phenomena.
As far as the annotation phase of the Parallel–TUT is concerned, it can be currently considered as concluded and the corpus will be soon released and made available for research purpose. In the next section, we describe the alignment phase which is the less advanced part of the project, currently under development.

5 Aligning the Parallel–TUT

Several techniques have been developed and made available for aligning texts at various granularities. They vary from document-structure to sentence, word, phrases or dependency subtrees (see e.g. (Wu, 2010; Li et al., 2010)).
Each level implies several and different issues that are currently in part unresolved also because does not exist an objective and universally shared notion of correspondence between sentence units. For instance, it is difficult to decide which words in a given target string correspond to which words in its source string (especially where idiomatic expressions are involved) and often, an alignment includes effects such as reorderings, omissions, insertions (Och and Ney, 2003).
Moreover, tools implementing aligment techniques are often designed with reference to some particular kind of annotation and schema, and cannot be applied to different formats, such as TUT. This is currently the major limit of the project that should be addressed in the next future. In fact, even if in our project we are interested in the alignment at various levels, we applied until now only some preliminary form of alignment, and the most of the time devoted to this part of the Parallel–TUT project has been spent in the analysis and report of the issues raised by our data.
First of all, the Parallel-TUT has been developed taking into account the issues related to the alignment at sentence and word level. Therefore, after the linguistic annotation, a further step has been the detection of lexical and structural correspondences between language pairs. As for the sentence level, the alignment was performed with Omega Aligner[13], a simple Python script used for the alignment of translation units within Computer Aided Translation (CAT) systems. The files produced conform to the Translation Memory eXchange (TMX) standard, an XML-compliant formatting standard normally used for storing and exchanging translation memories among CAT systems. Since the script expects the same number of segments in the source and target texts, some pre-processing was required, in order to avoid mismatches, in particular for punctuation marks.
As for the word alignment, considering the current absence of a tool which was compatible with the TUT format, the process was performed only preliminarily, using empirical methods, mainly in order to develop alignment guidelines that can drive the development of a tool suitable for such a task in the future. We observed that the alignment is made easier by the fact that languages are annotated using the same format, and because of TUT format strategy for the annotation of idiomatic expressions or compound words, which consists in splitting them in one line for each lexical word. In order to keep alignments as fine-grained as possible, two link types were designed to capture linguistic correspondences: exact and fuzzy. The former is used to identify complete and minimal semantic translation units, and the latter to indicate valid translation pairs (including all those cases of translation shifts). However, untranslated words, incorrect or deeply divergent translations are left unaligned.
At the same time, we chose to link correspondences at a structural level too, so that parallelisms between pairs of syntactic trees (or subtrees) could be easily detected and studied. In recent years, in fact, a number of syntactically motivated approaches to statistical machine translation have been proposed which focused on the fact that syntactic constituents tend to move as units with systematic differences in the word order of the languages involved (Zhang and Gildea, 2004). In the case of Parallel–TUT, a syntactically motivated alignment may be driven by the argument structure as annotated according to the TUT format. In particular, we planned to implement forms of alignment based on (a selection of the major) grammatical relations that are involved in the predicate argument structure, as figure 2 shows. We hypothesize that the features of the annotation schema of TUT can be of some help for the alignment at this granularity. Nevertheless, these features and the richness of the annotation schema of TUT are currently the major limits in the application of a standard tool for the alignment of the Parallel-TUT.

[13]http://www.omegat.org/en/resources.html

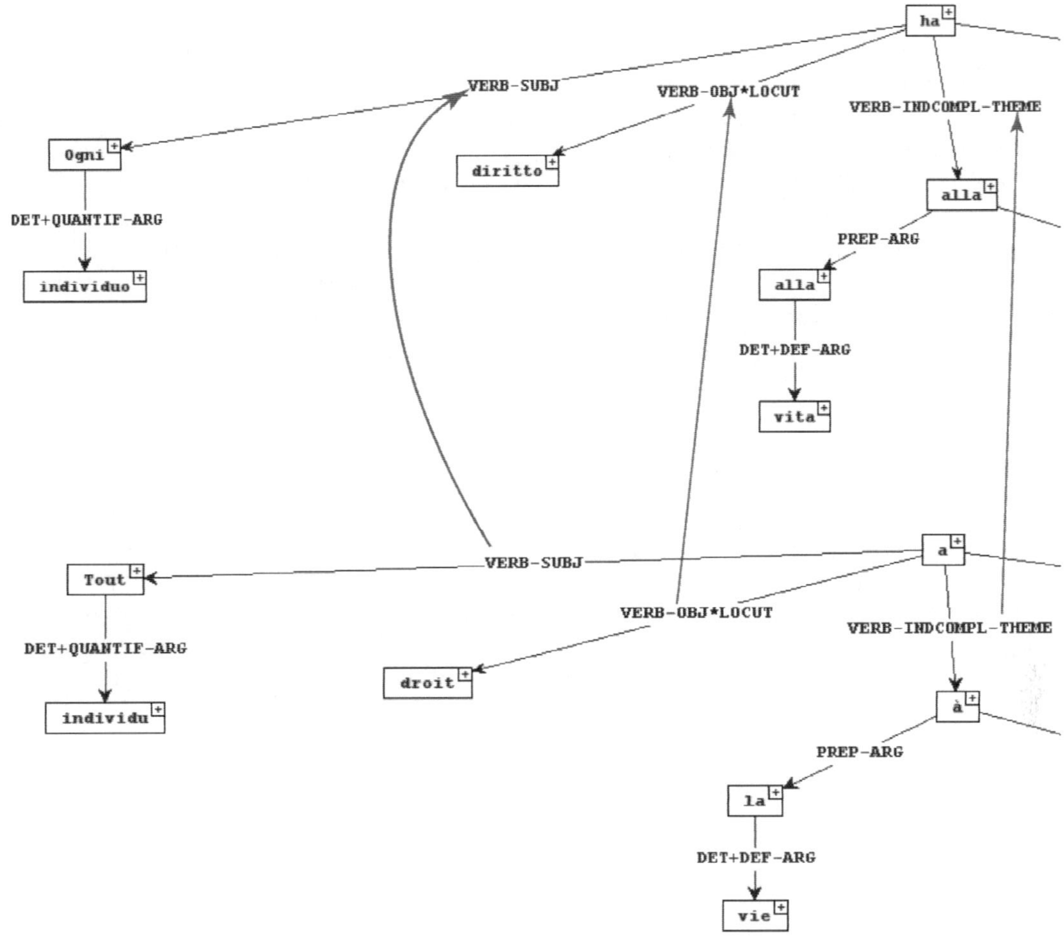

Figure 2: A sample of Italian-French alignment at dependency relation level in Parallel–TUT, for a fragment of the sentence "Ogni individuo ha diritto alla vita" (UDHR–ITA–20) – "Tout individu a droit à la vie" (UDHR–FR–19), corresponding to the UDHR–EN–21 for English: "Everyone has the right to life".

6 Discussion and future work

In this section we discuss the implications of applying the TUT format to English and French for the development of Parallel–TUT.

The first aspect we focused on, while evaluating our methodology and its effects, was the parser output, the type of errors produced and their investigation.

After the work phase described in Section 4, TULE, when evaluated according to its precision in building and labelling dependency trees, reached an error rate of around 9% for Italian, but 15,6% for English and 17,8% for French.

Errors detected during manual correction mainly dealt with tokenization and, to a larger extent, morphological analysis and Part of Speech tagging. This is maybe due to an incorrect application of disambiguation rules by the parser or to a lack of information about the lexical items in the TULE dictionary. As a result, these errors deeply affected the parser performance, and, despite rule-insertion operations, its output quality for English and French languages is still lower if compared to Italian. This suggests that further improvements in the system are required.

In addition to these errors, two other types have been identified. For their special character, we could define them as as " language-dependent" and "genre-dependent" errors. In the first case, errors have to do with the distinctive feature of each language. The most frequent phenomenon (among those encountered in our corpus) included in the former is that of the pre-modification in English, ie. all those cases of noun phrases where one or more units preceding the head of the phrase are syntactic modifiers of the head itself[14] structured in a hierarchic order. Since Italian language prefers post-modification, a parser trained for such linguistic patterns, in most cases, is unable to recognize the appropriate syntactic order between the units of the pre-modification.

As for the second type of errors, defined here as "genre-dependent", we include all those cases of errors directly attributable to the genre of the texts collected and analyzed in our small corpus. As we said, the collection comprises legal documents, where the recurrence of complex and ambiguous syntactic constructions (a feature shared by the three languages considered) is quite common. The high number of embedded prepositional phrases, subordinate clauses and parentheticals contributes to the lowering of the output quality.

As for the application of the TUT format and schema to the other two languages, distinctive features of these linguistic systems result in a lack of an appropriate structural representation, for which new relational labels were introduced, as described in Section 4. We tackled this problem with the two-fold goal of providing a coherent framework of annotation (like for Italian[15]), and taking into account the linguistic peculiarities of each language. This was made possible by a number of factors. First, the choice of a dependency (rather than constituent) structure better suits for both morphologically rich languages (such as Italian and French) and morphologically simpler ones (English). Moreover, the richness of relations provided in the TUT scheme, in addition to the use of null elements, which is another feature of the TUT format, allows a flexible annotation and the coverage of those linguistic phenomena which distinguish French and English from Italian (to name a few, the relative superlative in French, or the possessive case in English, as already mentioned in Section 4).

[14]This can be noticed, in the annotated texts, by the higher frequency of nominal modifiers (expressed by the NOUN-RMOD label) in English texts, rather than in the French and Italian sub-parts of the corpus; the occurences of such relation are 103 in English texts, 25 in the French and 17 in the Italian ones, covering respectively 2.5%, 0.5% and 0.4% of the total amount of relational labels.

[15]See the *linguistic notes* of TUT at `http://www.di.unito.it/ tutreeb/documents/noteling-engl-15-11-08.pdf`

As said at the beginning, the Parallel–TUT is currently an ongoing project, and the aim of the present work is mainly at raising and investigating issues related to its development. Nevertheless, in this phase of our project we observed that using the same format, and the TUT format in particular, has proved useful in the detection of similarities during the alignment phase at all the levels currently taken into account. The decision to adopt the same annotation scheme and grammatical description for the three languages can also contribute to the comparison of grammatical patterns.

As for future development of this work, a number of issues must be further pursued.

First of all, by taking into account the directions collected in the alignment guidelines developed during this first phase of the Parallel–TUT project, we will address the development and the integration of suitable tools, in particular for the alignment at the predicative structure level and for displaying such kind of information.

Secondly, considering the opportunity of converting TUT into a Penn-like format, we can extend the conversion to our parallel treebank as well, in order to develop alignment procedures also for phrases and information expressed in constituency-based formats.

Thirdly, in order to address the languages involved beyond the limits of a toy domain, it is crucial to enlarge the corpus of the Parallel–TUT. On the one hand, applying to a larger corpus our methodology to a larger corpus will give us the opportunity for addressing a larger and more meaningful set of linguistic phenomena typical of French and English, thouh not represented in Italian. On the other hand, this will allow more detailed analyses, like e.g. in (Ahrenberg, 2010), not affected by the sparseness of data that can be currently detected using our small corpus.

Finally, we observe that currently our corpus covers a selection of texts from a specific linguistic subfield broadly corresponding to legal language; one of the main future tasks should therefore consist not only in extending the size of the annotated corpus, but also in orienting to a more balanced direction its further development, comprising different sources, e.g. technical and specialized texts, fiction, newspapers (Paulussen and Macken, 2010).

7 Conclusions

In this paper we presented preliminary results in the creation of Parallel–TUT, a multilingual parallel treebank for Italian, English and French represented in the format of the Italian resource TUT. The project mainly aims at testing the hypothesis that the annotation schema and the knowledge annotated in the TUT format can be useful also to address the issues related to parallel corpora. Therefore, the same parsing system and the tools used for the improvement of the quality of the data annotated within TUT have been extended and applied to the other two languages.
Although this attempt has produced encouraging results, the project is currently ongoing and we presented several directions for its further development, extension and improvement.

References

L. Ahrenberg, J. Tiedemann, and M. Volk, editors. 2010. *Proceedings of the Workshop on Annotation and Exploitation of Parallel Corpora (AEPC)*. NEALT, Tartu.

L. Ahrenberg. 2007. LinEs: an English-Swedish Parallel Treebank. In *Proceedings of the 16th Nordic Conference on Computational Linguistics (NODALIDA '07)*, Tartu.

L. Ahrenberg. 2010. Clause restructuring in English-Swedish translation. In *Proceedings of the (AEPC)*, Tartu.

J. Bos, C. Bosco, and A. Mazzei. 2009. Converting a dependency treebank to a Categorial Grammar treebank for Italian. In *Proceedings of the 8th workshop on Treebanks and Linguistic Theories (TLT-8)*, Milan.

C. Bosco and A. Lavelli. 2010. Annotation schema-oriented validation for dependency parsing evaluation. In *Proceedings of the 9th workshop on Treebanks and Linguistic Theories (TLT-9)*, Tartu.

C. Bosco, A. Mazzei, and V. Lombardo. 2007. Evalita Parsing Task: an analysis of the first parsing system contest for Italian. *Intelligenza artificiale*, 2(IV).

C. Bosco, A. Mazzei, and V. Lombardo. 2009a. Evalita'09 Parsing Task: constituency parsers and the Penn format for Italian. In *Proceedings of Evalita'09*, Reggio Emilia.

C. Bosco, S. Montemagni, A. Mazzei, V. Lombardo, F. Dell'Orletta, and A. Lenci. 2009b. Evalita'09 Parsing Task: comparing dependency parsers and treebanks. In *Proceedings of Evalita'09*, Reggio Emilia.

C. Bosco. 2007. Multiple-step treebank conversion: from dependency to Penn format. In *Proceedings of the Linguistic Annotation Workshop (LAW) at ACL'07*, Prague.

L. Cyrus. 2006. Building a Resource for Studying Translation Shifts. In *Proceedings of Language Resources and Evaluation Conference (LREC'06)*, Genova.

S. Grimes, X. Li, A. Bies, S. Kulick, X. Ma, and S. Strassel. 2010. Creating arabic-english parallel word-aligned treebank corpora at LDC. In *Proceedings of Language Resources and Evaluation Conference (LREC'10)*, Malta.

J. Hajič and P. Zemánek. 2003. Prague Arabic Dependency Treebank: Development in data and tools. In *Proceedings of NEMLAR the NEMLAR Conference on Arabic Language Resources and Tools*, Cairo.

R. Hudson. 1984. *Word grammar*. Basil Blackwell, Oxford and New York.

N. Klyueva and D. Mareček. 2010. Towards Parallel Czech-Russian Dependency Treebank. In *Proceedings of the Workshop on Annotation and Exploitation of Parallel Corpora (AEPC)*, Tartu.

L. Lesmo, V. Lombardo, and C. Bosco. 2002. Treebank development: the TUT approach. In *Proceedings of ICON02*, Mumbay.

L. Lesmo. 2007. The rule-based parser of the NLP group of the University of Torino. *Intelligenza artificiale*, 2(IV).

L. Lesmo. 2009. The Turin University Parser at Evalita 2009. In *Proceedings of Evalita'09*, Reggio Emilia.

X. Li, S. Strassel, S. Grimes, S. Ismael, X. Ma, N. Ge, A. Bies, N. Xue, and M. Maamouri. 2010. Parallel aligned treebank corpora at LDC: Methodology, annotation and integration. In *Proceedings of Workshop on Annotation and Exploitation of Parallel Corpora (AEPC)*, Tartu.

B. Megyesi, B. Dahlqvist, E. Pettersson, and J. Nivre. 2008. Swedish-Turkish Parallel Treebank. In *Proceedings of Language Resources and Evaluation Conference (LREC'08)*, Marrakech.

G. Musillo and K. Sima'an. 2002. Towards comparing parsers from different linguistic frameworks. An information theoretic approach. In *Proceedings of Workshop Beyond PARSEVAL - Towards improved evaluation measures for parsing systems at the LREC'02*, Las Palmas.

F. J. Och and H. Ney. 2003. A systematic comparison of various statistical alignment models. *Computational Linguistics*, 29(1).

H. Paulussen and L. Macken. 2010. Annotating the Dutch Parallel Corpus. In *Proceedings of the Workshop on Annotation and Exploitation of Parallel Corpora (AEPC)*, Tartu.

A. Rios, A. Ghring, and M. Volk. 2009. A Quechua–Spanish parallel treebank. In *Proceedings of 7th Workshop on Treebanks and Linguistic Theories (TLT-7)*, Groningen.

R. Steinberger, B. Pouliquen, A. Widiger, C. Ignat, T. Erjavec, D. Tufiş, and D Varga. 2006. The JRC-Acquis: A multilingual aligned parallel corpus with 20+ languages. In *Proceedings of Language Resources and Evaluation Conference (LREC'06)*, Genova.

M. Čmejrek, J. Hajič, and V. Kuboň. 2004. Prague Czech-English Dependency Treebank: Syntactically Annotated Resources for Machine Translation. In *Proceedings of EAMT 10th Annual Conference*, Budapest.

M. Volk, A. Göhring, T. Marek, and Y. Samuelsson. 2010. SMULTRON (version 3.0) - The Stockholm MULtilingual parallel TReebank. An English-French-German-Spanish-Swedish parallel treebank with sub-sentential alignments.

D. Wu. 2010. Alignment. In *Handbook of NLP*. Chapmand and Hale/CRC Press.

H. Zhang and D. Gildea. 2004. Syntax-based alignment: Supervised or unsupervised? In *Proceedings of COLING'04*, Geneve.

Bulgarian-English Parallel Treebank: Word and Semantic Level Alignment

Kiril Simov
LMD, IICT-BAS
kivs@bultreebank.org

Petya Osenova
LMD, IICT-BAS
petya@bultreebank.org

Laska Laskova
LMD, IICT-BAS
laska@bultreebank.org

Aleksandar Savkov
LMD, IICT-BAS
savkov@bultreebank.org

Stanislava Kancheva
LMD, IICT-BAS
stanislava@bultreebank.org

Abstract

The paper describes the basic strategies behind the word and semantic level alignment in the Bulgarian-English treebank. The word level alignment has taken into consideration the experience within other NLP groups in the context of the Bulgarian language specific features. The semantic level alignment builds on the word level alignment and is represented in the framework of the Minimal Recursion Semantics.

1 Introduction

Manually created aligned bi- or multilingual corpora have proven to be useful resources in variety of tasks, e.g. for the development of automatic alignment tools, but also for lexicon extraction, word sense disambiguation, machine translation, annotation transfer and others.

In this paper we describe the word level alignment of the Bulgarian-English Parallel HPSG Treebank (BulEngTreebank) and its connection to the semantic level alignment. The aim of constructing such a treebank is to use it as a source for learning of statistical transfer rules for Bulgarian-English machine translation along the lines of (Bond et al. 2011 to appear). The transfer rules in this framework are rewriting rules over MRS (Minimal Recursion Semantics) structures. The basic format of the transfer rules is:

$$[C:]\ I\ [!F] \rightarrow O$$

where *I* is the *input* of the rule, *O* is the *output*. *C* determines the *context* and *F* is the *filter* of the rule. *C* selects positive context and *F* selects negative context for the application of a rule. For more details on the transfer rules consult (Oepen 2008). This type of rules allows for the extremely flexible transfer of factual and linguistic knowledge between the source and the target languages. Thus the treebank has to contain parallel sentences, their syntactic and semantic analyses and correspondences on the level of MRS.

In the development of such a parallel treebank we rely on the Bulgarian HPSG resource grammar BURGER, and on a dependency parser (Malt Parser – Nivre et al. 2006), trained on the BulTreeBank data. Both parsers produce semantic representations in terms of MRS. The treebank is a parallel resource aligned first on a sentence level. Then the alignment is done on the level of MRS. This level of abstraction makes possible the usage of different tools for producing these alignments, since MRS is meant to be compatible with various syntactic frameworks. The chosen procedure is as follows: first, the Bulgarian sentences are parsed with BURGER. If it succeeds, then the produced MRSes are used for the alignment. In case BURGER fails, the sentences are parsed with Malt Parser, and then MRSes are constructed on the base of the dependency analysis. The latter MRSes are created via a set of transfer rules (see Simov and Osenova 2011). In both cases we keep the syntactic analyses for the parallel sentences.

With respect to the MRS alignments, a very pragmatic approach has been adopted – namely, the MRS alignments originated from the word level alignment. This approach is based on the following observations and requirements:

Proceedings of Recent Advances in Natural Language Processing, pages 29–38,
Hissar, Bulgaria, 12-14 September 2011.

- Both approaches for generation of MRS over the sentences are lexicalized;
- Non-experts in linguistics can do the alignments successfully on word level;
- Different rules for generation/testing are possible.

Both parsers (for Bulgarian and English), which we use for the creation of MRSes, are lexicalized in their nature. Thus, they first assign elementary predicates to the lexical elements in the sentences, and then, on the base of the syntactic analysis, these elementary predicates are composed into MRSes for the corresponding phrases, and finally of the whole sentence.

Our belief is that having alignments on word level, syntactic analyses and the rules for composition of MRS, we will be able to determine correspondences between bigger MRSes than only lexical level MRSes, using the ideas of (Tinsley et al, 2009). They first establish the mapping on word level (automatically), then for candidate phrases they calculate the rank of the correspondences on the base of the word level alignment. Thus, our idea is to score the correspondences between two MRSes on the base of involved elementary predicates as well as the syntactic structure of the parallel sentences.

As it was mentioned, the alignment on word level allows us to do more reliable alignments using annotators who are non-experts in linguistics. Currently, the inter-annotator agreement is 92 %. Also this kind of alignment does not require any initial knowledge of MRS from the annotators. Another advantage is that the result might be used for training tools for automatic word alignment, and thus automatic extension of the treebank can be performed. Additionally, the word level alignment might be done before the actual analysis of the sentences. This is especially useful in case of Bulgarian, where the BURGER grammar is underdeveloped in comparison with the English grammar.

The paper is structured as follows: the next section discusses the related works on word alignment strategies. Section 3 focuses on the basic principles behind the word alignment between Bulgarian and English. Section 4 describes the level of MRS alignments. Section 5 outlines the conclusions.

2 Previous Work on Word Level Alignment

The annotation guidelines for Bulgarian-English word alignment, presented here, gained from the tradition established by the guidelines used in similar projects, aiming at the creation of golden standards for different language pairs, such as the Blinker project for English-French alignment (Melamed 1998), the alignment task for the Prague Czech-English Dependency Treebank 1.0 (Kruijff-Korbayová et al. 2006), the Dutch parallel Corpus project (Macken 2010), among others.

As Lambert et al. (2006) point out, the alignment decisions presented in the guidelines reflect different tasks. There are projects such as ARCADE (Vèronis, 2000) and PLUG (Ahrenberg et al., 2000), which aim at building a reference corpora with word, not sentence pairs, and have a different annotation strategy in contrast to those that focus on sentence level. Different linguistic theoretical backgrounds appear to be another source of divergence that affects the rules of phrase alignments as well as the specific grammatical techniques. This holds especially in correspondences between synsemantic words (like prepositions, determiners, particles, auxiliary verbs) and synsemantic and/or autosemantic words (Macken 2010). In addition, some tools for manual word alignment, e.g. HandAlign[1], allow the user to link both phrases and their elements with different kind of links, which might be simulated in other tools, which are more restrictive. Finally, the use of the so called possible (also ambiguous, fuzzy or weak) links that signal correspondence between semantically and/or structurally nonequivalent words or phrases is also a matter of dispute. While some argue that alignment with possible links should be determined by unambiguous rules, formulated with consideration of inter-annotation agreement, others (Lambert et al. 2006) allow for different decisions to be kept, which is true to the role originally ascribed to this kind of links: "P (possible) alignment which is used for alignments which might or might not exist" (Och and Ney 2000).

3 Word Level Alignment

The word level alignment was performed by the **WordAligner**[2] – a web-based tool for word alignment, built on top of the word alignment interface developed by C. Callison-Burch. It allows the user to provide parallel input of non-aligned text through the interface or to upload file(s) with sentence level aligned texts. Editing and/or completion of alignments is also supported. Each pair

[1] Available at http://www.cs.utah.edu/~hal/HandAlign/

[2] http://www.bultreebank.bas.bg/aligner/index.php

of sentences is represented as a grid of squares (Fig. 1). For convenience English is considered to be the *source* and Bulgarian – the *target* language, but that has no implications for the translation direction. Correspondence between two tokens is marked by clicking on a square – once (black square) or twice (dark grey square). Originally, the two colours were introduced to allow the annotator to mark his/her degree of certainty about the alignment decision: *sure link* (S link, black) or *possible link* (P link, dark grey). It is worth noting that in an alignment there can be only one type of link between two tokens or, more precisely, there is no distinction between phrase and word levels.

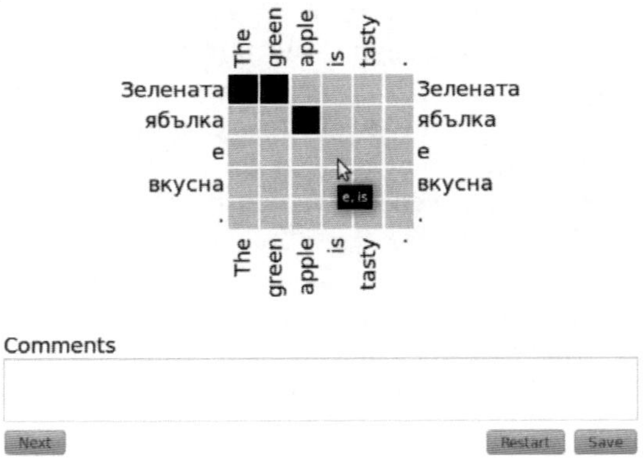

Fig 1. *Aligner interface. Mapping is done by clicking on the squares.*

Subsequently the colours were used to distinguish between *strong* and *weak* alignment (Kruijff-Korbayová et al. 2006), thus P link (dark grey) represents either *weak* alignment, or that the annotator is *uncertain* about the pairing, or both. S link (black) represents either *strong* alignment, or that the annotator is *certain* about the pairing, or both.

General rules

We adopt the general rules that have proven to be shared by the different annotation tasks and alignment strategies. The number of corresponding tokens to be aligned can be estimated by following these two rules (Veronis 1998, Merkel 1999, Macken 2010):

1. Mark as many tokens as necessary in the source and in the target sentence to ensure a two-way equivalence.
2. Mark as few tokens as possible in the source and in the target sentence, but preserve the two-way equivalence.

If a token or a phrase has no corresponding counterpart in the other language and bears no structural and/or semantic significance, it should be left unlinked (NULL link, square with no fill) (Melamed 1998).

Idioms and free translations present a special case. If two autosemantic words or phrases refer to the same object, but do not share the same meaning, they are aligned with a P link, e.g.:

(1) *this animal*
това куче ['this dog']

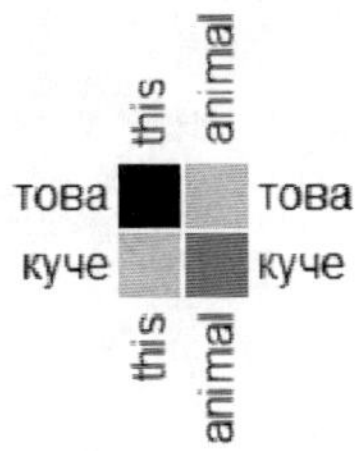

The same rule holds when there is a synsemantic – autosemantic correspondence:

(2) ***Ivan 's*** *mother called.*
Неговата *майка се обади.* ['His mother called.']

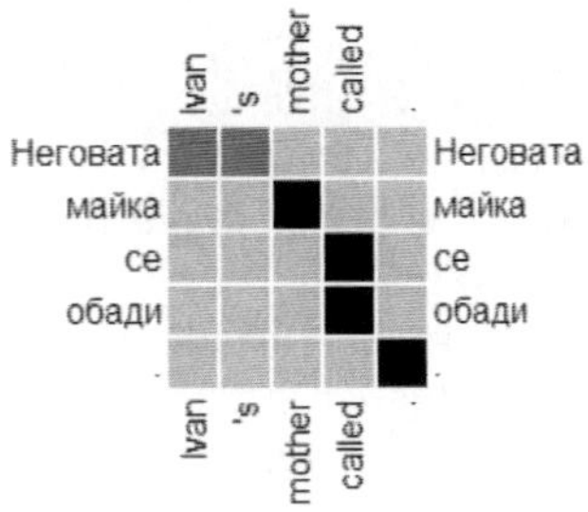

P link: *Ivan 's ~ Неговата*

P link is used when a lexical item is paraphrased in the other language:

(3) *these non-Serbs*
тези лица от несръбски произход ['persons from a non-Serbian origin']

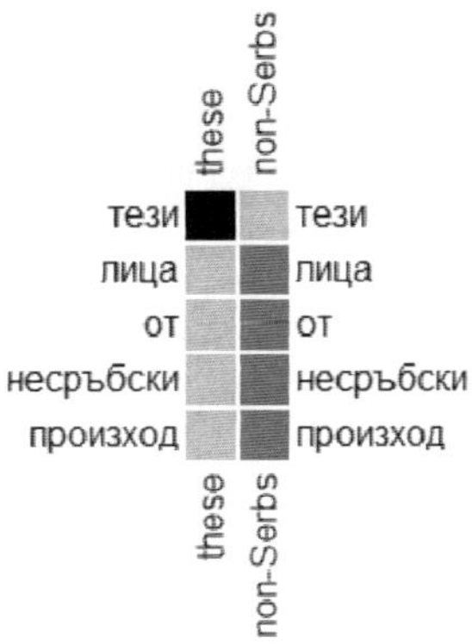

P link: *non-Serbs ~ лица от несръбски произход*

Idioms are linked with an S link; each token from the idiom in the source sentence is aligned with each token from the idiom in the target sentence.

(4) *She'll marry him* ***when pigs begin to fly****.*
Тя ще се омъжи за него ***на куково лято****.*

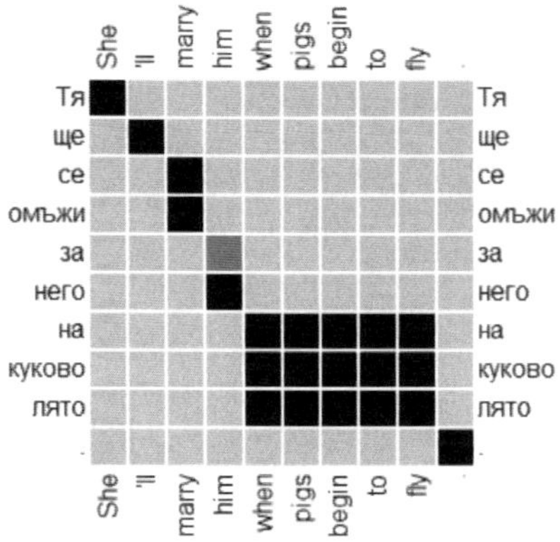

S link: *when pigs begin to fly* ~ *на куково лято*

Specific rules

These rules are primarily language specific and their subjects are predominantly function words (prepositions, determiners, auxiliary verbs and the like). We give preference to the semantic equivalence where possible.

Noun phrases

Determiners. Articles, demonstratives and possessive pronouns

a) English determiners like *a(n)* or *the* correspond either to Bulgarian determiners *един* [one] (always in preposition, see example (7), or bare NP (5), or to the so called full/short definite article (6). In both languages they are attached to the first modifier of the NP, if there is one, regardless of its position[3].

(5) *I live in **a house**.*
*Живея в **къща**.*

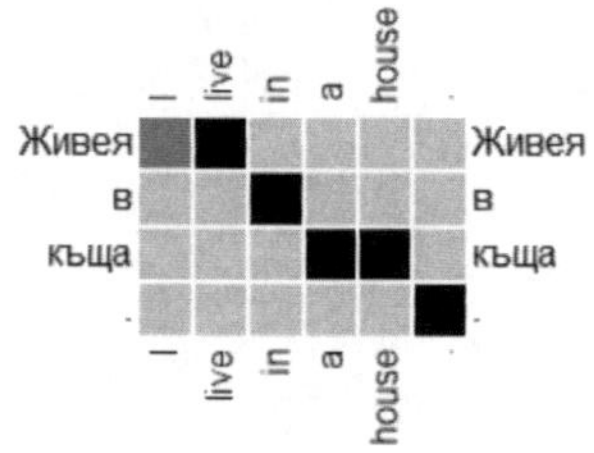

S link: *a house* ~ *къща*

(6) *Look at **the house**!*
*Виж **къщата**!*

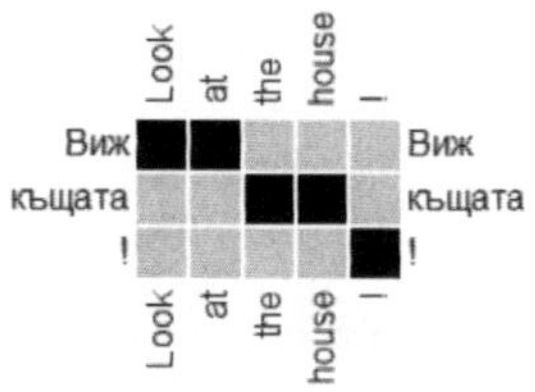

S link: ***the** house* ~ *къща**та***

[3] There are some exceptions in Bulgarian, e.g. *хубави **едни** дечица* ('pretty ones children' – some pretty children). In this case *едни* and *some* should be surely aligned.

(7) *I saw **a house** at the hill.*
*Видях **една къща** на хълма.*

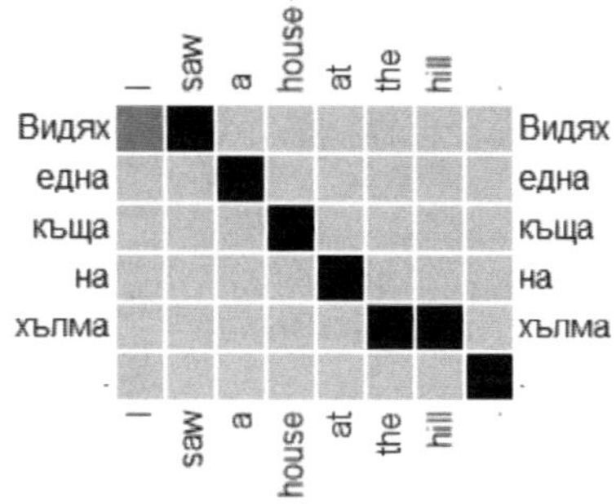

S link: *a* ~ *една*

S link: *house* ~ *къща*

b) Usually if one of the two corresponding NPs has no modifier, the determiner and the head of the phrase are aligned together to the head of the other phrase (compare for example the rules presented in Kruijff-Korbayová 2006 or Macken 2010). Since in Bulgarian the article could be a morpheme attached to the first modifier (8), we decided to link both the article and the modifier from the English sentence to the corresponding Bulgarian modifier with an S link.

(8) ***the** lovely old house*
*хубава**та** стара къща*

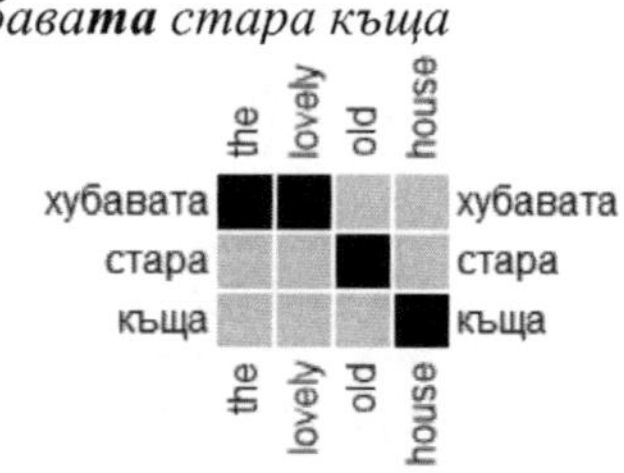

S link: *the lovely* ~ *хубава**та***

S link: *house* ~ *къща*

c) We follow (Kruijff-Korbayová 2006) in linking determiners from different word classes, based on the similarity in their function. Thus the correspondence between indefinite articles and indefinite pronouns is marked with an S link (9).

(9) *a girl*
някакво момиче

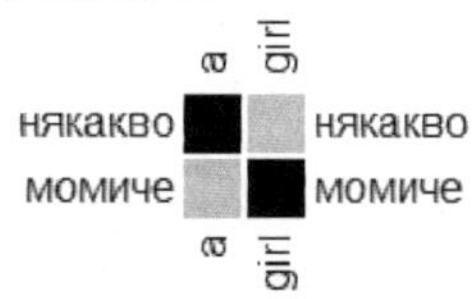

S link: *a* ~ *някакво*

S link: *girl* ~ *момиче*

d) English definite articles and Bulgarian demonstrative pronouns are also aligned with an S link (10).

(10) *the man*
този човек

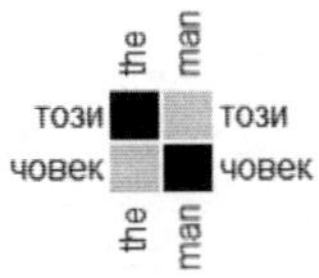

S link: *the ~ този*

S link: *man ~ човек*

e) We use P link to align *the* with definite forms of full possessive pronouns (11) because the possesive.

(11) *I heard* ***the*** *words,*
Чух ***техните*** *думи.*

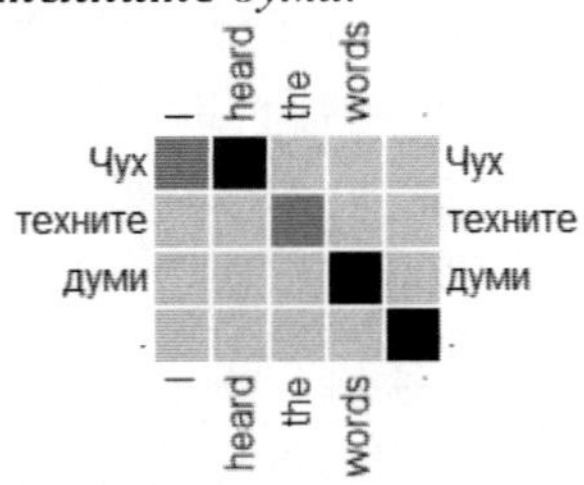

P link: *the ~ техните*

S link: *words ~ думи*

Substitution with *one(s)*

Both lexical substitution and nominalization with the numeral *one(s)*, which are typical for English, have no structural and semantic analogy in Bulgarian. They should be aligned to the Bulgarian lexical unit that correspond to the premodifier of *one* (12), or, if there isn't any, to the coreferential Bulgarian pronoun (13).

(12) *the little ones*
малките

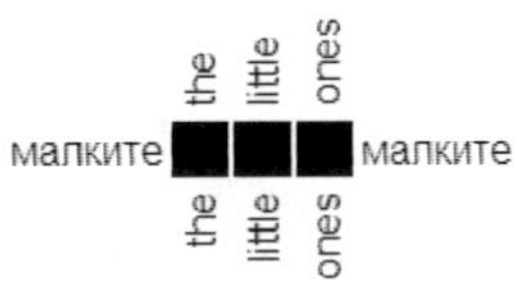

(13) ***the ones*** *that we love*
онези*, които обичаме*

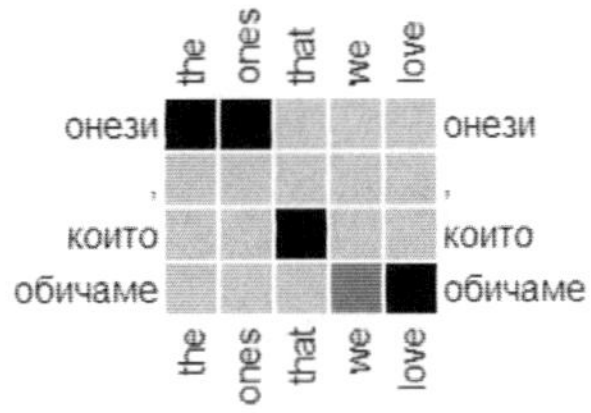

Prepositional phrases

a) Very often English noun premodifiers are translated into prepositional phrases in Bulgarian (14). If that is the case, the preposition is aligned with a P link to the head noun, for example:

(14) ***Justice*** *Minister Cemil Cicek*
Министърът ***на правосъдието*** *Джемил Чичек*

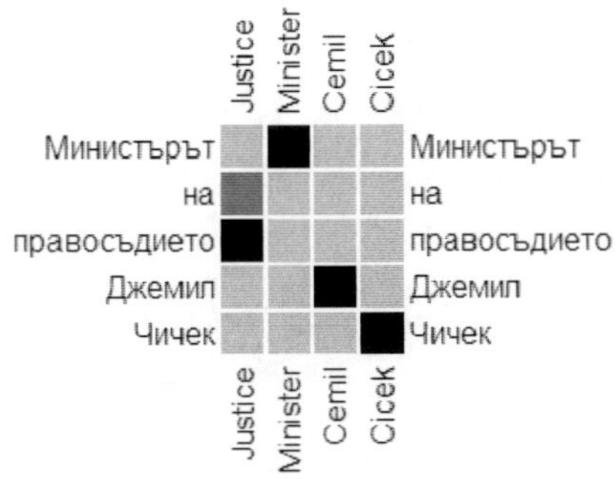

S link: *Justice ~ правосъдието*

P link: *Justice ~ на*

b) English possessive noun forms are translated into Bulgarian either with *на* prepositional phrase (*John's* – ***на*** *Иван*), or with an adjective that has possessive meaning (*John's* – *Иванов*). In case of PP translation, the preposition itself is aligned to the possessive ***'s*** (for singular) or ***'*** (for plural) marker with an P link to reflect the fact that the two possessive markers are morphosyntactically different (15).

(15) ***JNA's*** *1st Guards Motorised Brigade*
Първа гвардейска моторизирана бригада ***на ЮНА***

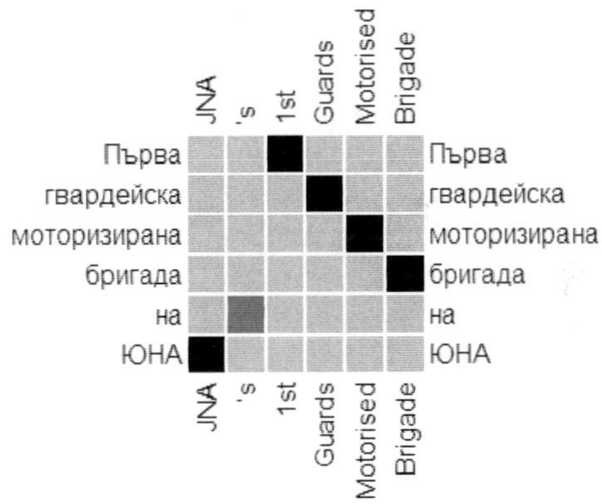

S link: *JNA ~ ЮНА*

P link: *'s ~ на*

Verb forms

We follow the rules as they were first formulated in (Melamed 1998): link main verb to main verb and auxiliary verb(s) to auxiliary verb(s) if possible. Whenever the auxiliary form is not present or different in the source or target phrase, it should be aligned to the main verb (see for example (19), weakly or the two verb forms should be phrase aligned (21).

Expletive subject and pro-drop

a) Expletive subjects (*it, there*) usually have no correspondence in Bulgarian sentences, but they are obligatory for English. That is why we decided to link them with an S link to all Bulgarian verb components, i.e. to the whole verb complex.

(16) *It is raining.*
Вали.

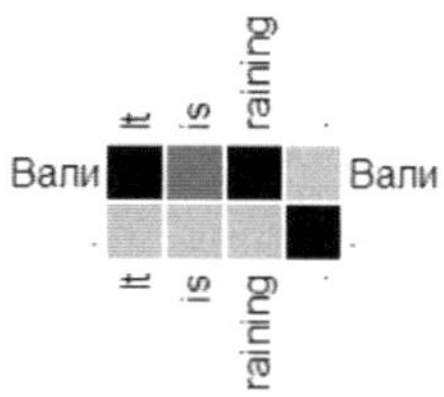

S link: *It ~ Вали*

(17) ***there are** many things*
***има** много неща*

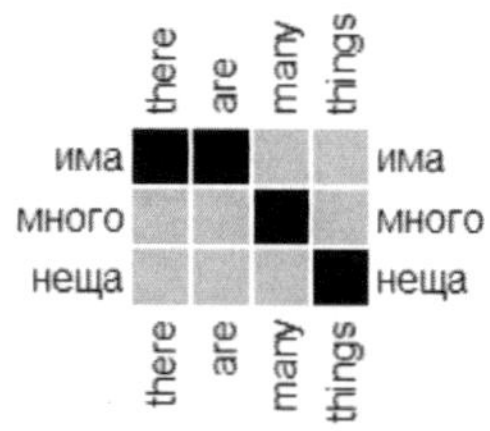

S link: *there are ~ има*

b) Bulgarian language is a pro-drop language. If the subject is unexpressed (18, 19, 20), then the English subject should be linked with a P link to all Bulgarian verb components that express one of the agreement categories: person, gender, number, and the main verb form itself. This decision is similar to the decision described in (Lambert et al. 2006) concerning the correspondences between English and Spanish verb phrases with omitted subjects.

(18) *He knows*
Знае

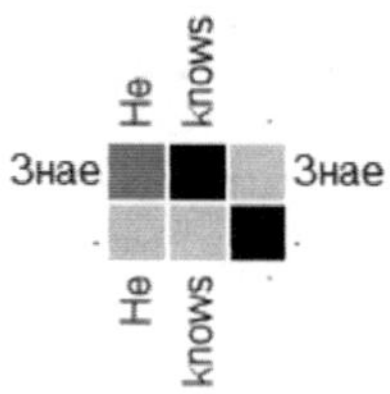

P link: *He ~ Знае*

(19) *She was not crying.*
Не плачеше.

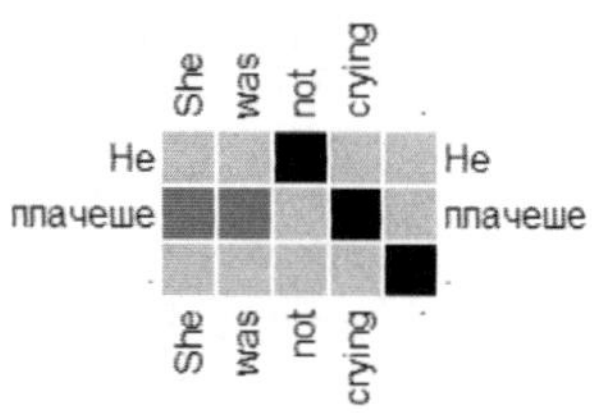

P link: *She ~ плачеше*

(20) *They would not dare.*
Не биха посмели.

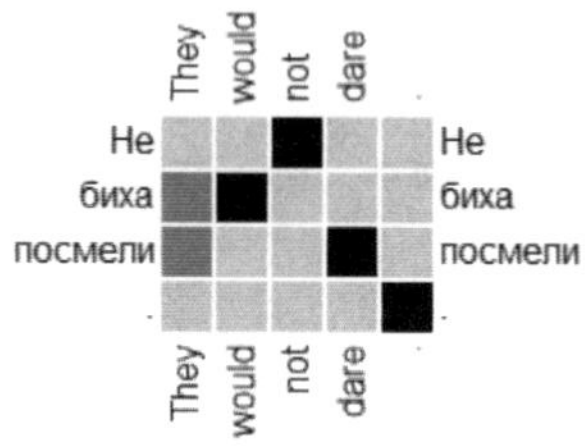

P link: *They ~ биха*
P link: *They ~ посмели*

Reflexive pronouns in a verb complex

a) Reflexive Bulgarian *се* and *си* particles may be part of the verb lemma (21, 22). If that is the case, they should be aligned with an S link to the non-reflexive English verb form.

(21) *had **met** earlier*
*бяхме **се срещнали** по-рано*

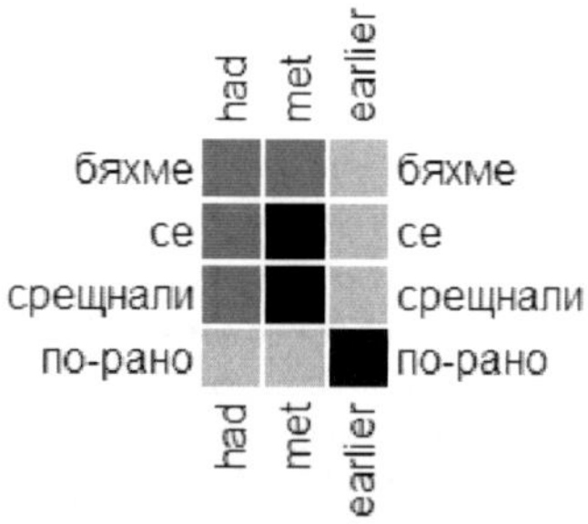

S link: *met ~ се срещнали*

b) In contrast to the rules construed for Czech-English alignments (Kruijff-Korbayová 2006), if the reflexive particle is used to form a passive voice construction, it is aligned to the English verb phrase as a whole with a P link. The difference is due to the fact that although we also align the verb forms as phrases, we try to mark separately the correspondence between the main verbs.

(22) *the house **is being built***
*къщата **се строи***

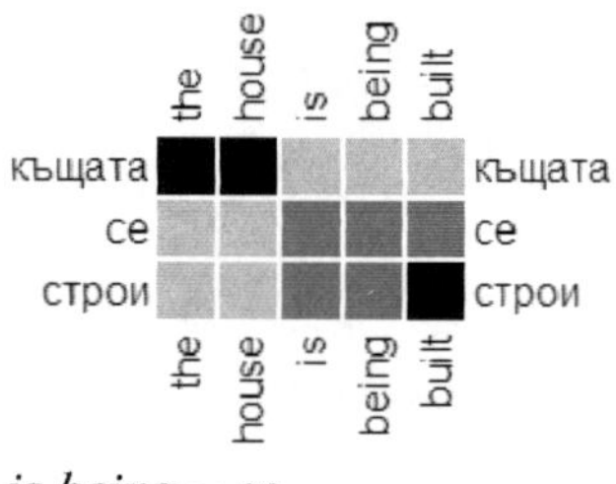

S link: *is being ~ се*
S link: *built ~ строи*

***To* and *да* particles**

a) The correspondence between *to* and *да* is usually pretty straightforward.

(23) *the decision **to** stay*
*решението **да** остана*

S link: *to ~ да*

b) In the case when *to* is not present in the source sentence, *да* should be linked with a P link to the English verb that is aligned to the Bulgarian verb following the particle. Not surprisingly this rule resembles the rule for aligning Dutch (*om*)...*te* constructions (Macken 2010) with English full infinitive or *-ing* forms – as a infinitival particle Bulgarian *да* occupies similar syntactic positions and has similar functions.

(24) *they stopped **yelling***
*те спряха **да викат***

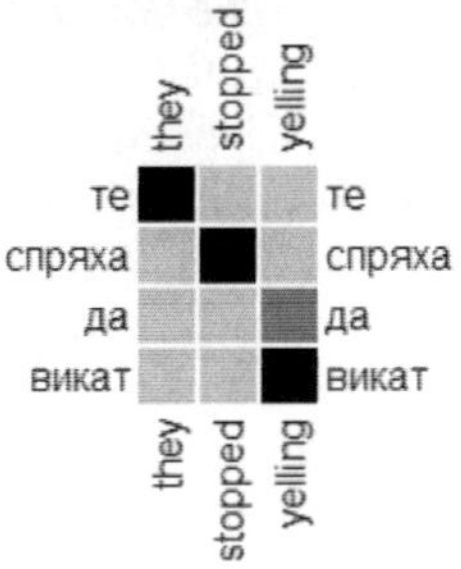

P link: *yelling ~ да*
S link: *yelling ~ викат*

(25) *they may **go***
*те може **да тръгват***

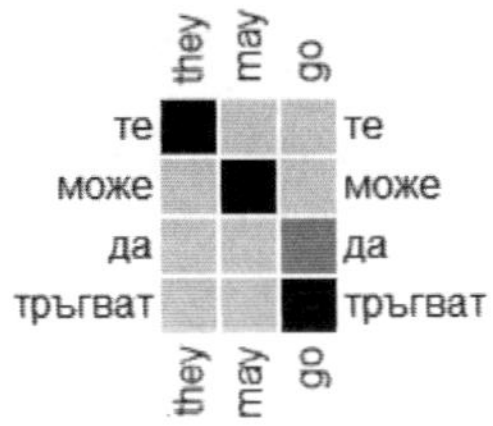

P link: *go ~ да*
S link: *go ~ тръгват*

(26) *You will not **perish**.*
*Ти няма **да загинеш**.*

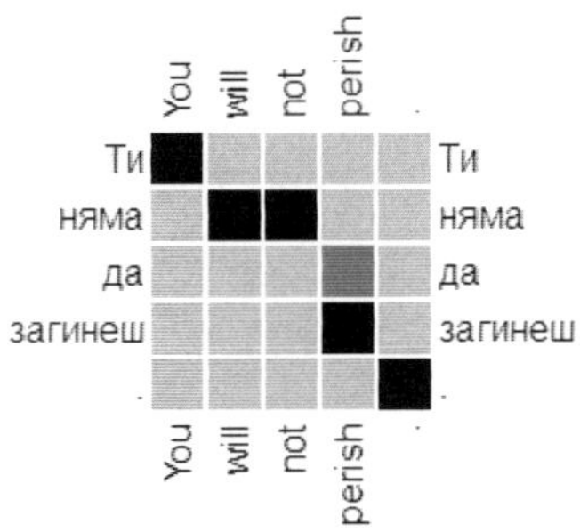

P link: *perish ~ да*
S link: *perish ~ загинеш*

Double negation

a) Double negation is typical for Slavic languages like Czech and Bulgarian, but not for English. In Czech the verb itself has a morphologically marked negative form that is weakly aligned with the positive form in English (Kruijff-Korbayová 2006). In Bulgarian the negative marker is not a morpheme, but a particle (*не,* 27) or an auxiliary verb with negative meaning (*няма, нямаше* 28). Often it is the case that one or more negative pronouns from the Bulgarian sentence correspond to indefinite English pronouns (27). They should be mapped with a P link.

(27) *I **couldn't** see **anything**.*
***Не можах** да видя **нищо**.*

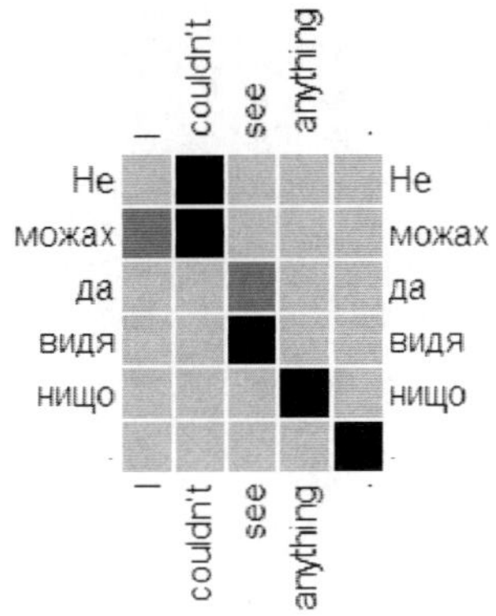

S link: *could'nt ~ не можах*
S link: *anything ~ нищо*

(28) *I **wouldn't** come.*
***Нямаше** да дойда.*

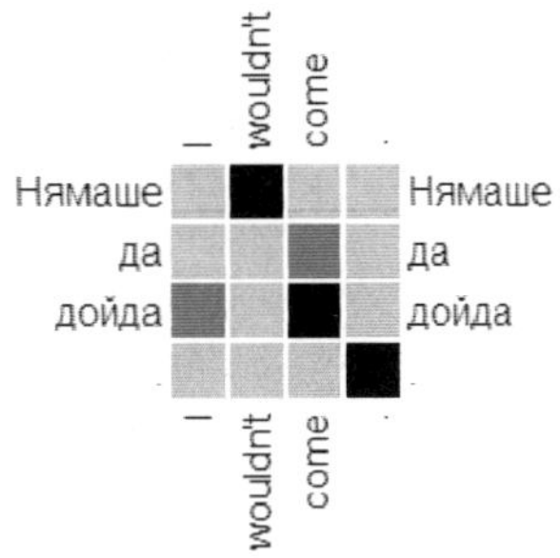

S link: *would n't ~ Нямаше*

If it is the English verb, that doesn't have negative form, then we use a P link to align the Bulgarian negative particle to the English word that bares negative meaning.

(29) *I felt nothing.*
Нищо не почувствах.

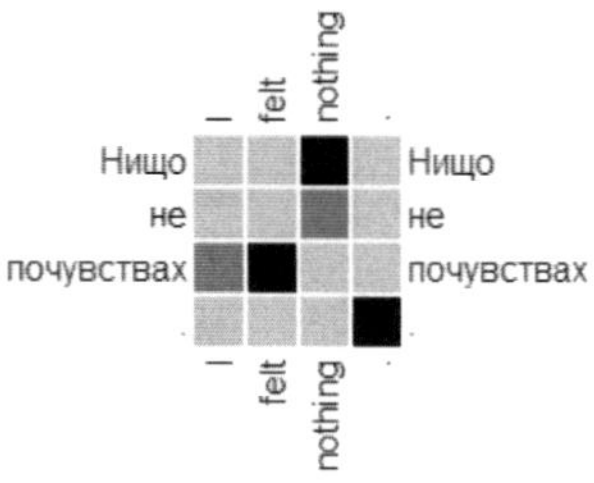

S link: *nothing ~ Нищо*
P link: *nothing ~ не*

Numerals

Cardinal and ordinal multiword numerals are treated as compound nouns and thus they are aligned as a block within which one-to-one correspondences are sure aligned (see for alternative decision Graça et al. 2008).

(30) ***one hundred and twenty two*** *men*
сто двайсет и двама *мъже*

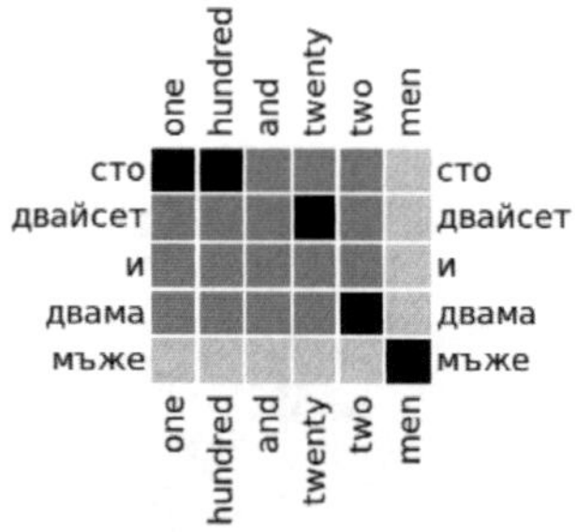

4 MRS Level Alignment

As it was mentioned above, we use the word level alignment in order to establish alignment on the level of MRS. For both languages the phrases are assigned an MRS structure which represents the semantic value of the phrase (in the case of dependency parse this MRS incorporates the semantic values of all dependent elements). The intuition behind our approach is that the lexical data of each structure in the syntactic analysis for a pair of sentences are aligned on word level. Then we assume that their MRS structures are equivalent modulo the meaning of the language specific elementary predicates. We exploit this intuition in constructing the semantic alignment in our treebank.

MRS is introduced as an underspecified semantic formalism (Copestake et al, 2005). It is used to support semantic analyses in HPSG English grammar – ERG (Copestake and Flickinger, 2000), but also in other grammar formalisms like LFG. The main idea is the formalism to rule out spurious analyses resulting from the representation of logical operators and the scope of quantifiers. Here we will present only basic definitions from (Copestake et al, 2005). For more details the cited publication should be consulted. An MRS structure is a tuple <*GT*, *R*, *C*>, where *GT* is the top handle, R is a bag of EPs (elementary predicates) and *C* is a bag of handle constraints, such that there is no handle *h* that outscopes *GT*. Each elementary predication contains exactly four components: (1) a handle which is the label of the EP; (2) a relation; (3) a list of zero or more ordinary variable arguments of the relation; and (4) a list of zero or more handles corresponding to scopal arguments of the relation (i.e., holes). Here is an example of an MRS structure for the sentence "*Every dog chases some white cat.*"

<h0, {h1: every(x,h2,h3), h2: dog(x), h4: chase(x, y), h5: some(y,h6,h7), h6: white(y), h6: cat(y)}, {}>

The top handle is *h0*. The two quantifiers are represented as relations *every(x, y, z)* and *some(x, y, z)* where *x* is the bound variable, *y* and *z* are handles determining the restriction and the body of the quantifier. The conjunction of two or more relations is represented by sharing the same handle (*h6* above). The outscope relation is defined as a transitive closure of the immediate outscope relation between two elementary predications – EP immediately outscopes EP' iff one of the scopal arguments of EP is the label of EP'. In this example the set of handle constraints is empty, which means that the representation is underspecified with respect to the scope of both quantifiers. Here we finish with the brief introduction of the MRS formalism.

First we establish correspondences on lexical level. Each two lexical items in the corresponding analyses are made equivalent on the basis of word alignment. Special attention is paid to the analytical verb forms and clitics. The next step is to traverse the trees in bottom-up manner. For each phrase or head for which the components are aligned, a correspondence on the MRS level is established. It should be explicitly noted that a correspondence on a sentence level is also established. Here we present an example:

Let us consider the following pair of sentences from the English Resource Grammar datasets:

Kucheto	na	Braun	lae.
Dog-the(neut)	of	Browne	barks.

Browne's dog barks.

The word level alignment is:

(***Kucheto = dog***)
(***na = 's***)
(***na Braun = Browne 's***)
(***lae = barks***)
(***Braun = Browne***)

Here are the MRS structures assigned to both sentences by ERG and BURGER. Some details are hidden for readability:

ERG:

<h1, { h3: proper_q_rel(x3,h4,h6),
h7: named_rel(x5,"Browne"),
h8: def_explicit_q_rel(x10, h9, h11),
h12: poss_rel(e13,x10,x5),
h12: dog_n_1_rel(x10),
h14: bark_v_1_rel(e2,x10)},
{ h4 qeq h7 h9 qeq h12 }>

BURGER:

<h1, { h3: kuche_n_1_rel(x4),
h3: na_p_1_rel(e5,x4,x6),
h7: named_rel(x6, "Braun"),
h8: exist_q_rel (x6, h9, h10),
h11: exist_q_rel (x4, h12, h13),
h1: laya_v_rel (e2,x4)},
{ h12 qeq h3 h9 qeq h7 }>

The result of correspondences between MRS on the basis of word level establishes the following mappings of elementary predicates lists:

(m1)

(***Braun*** = ***Browne***)

{ h3: proper_q_rel(x5, h4, h6),
h7: named_rel(x5, "Browne") }

to

{ h7: named_rel(x6, "Braun"),
h8: exist_q_rel(x6, h9, h10) }

(m2)

(***na*** = ***'s***)

{ h12: poss_rel(e13, x10, x5) }

to

{ h3: na_p_1_rel(e5, x4, x6) }

(m3)

(***na Braun*** = ***Browne 's***)

{ h3: proper_q_rel(x5, h4, h6),
h7: named_rel(x5, "Browne"),
h8: def_explicit_q_rel(x10, h9, h11),
h12: poss_rel(e13, x10, x5) }

to

{ h3: na_p_1_rel(e5, x4, x6),
h7: named_rel(x6, "Braun"),
h8: exist_q_rel(x6, h9, h10) }

(m4)

(***Kucheto*** = ***dog***)

{ h12: dog_n_1_rel(x10) }

to

{ h3: kuche_n_1_rel(x4),
h11: exist_q_rel(x4, h12, h13) }

(m5)

(***lae*** = ***barks***)

{ h14: bark_v_1_rel(e2, x10) }

to

{ h1: laya_v_rel(e2, x4) }

As we mentioned above, our goal is to have MRS alignment not just on word level, but also on phrase level in the sentence. Thus, using the correspondences described in the previous section and the syntactic analyses of both sentences we can infer the following mapping:

(m6)

(***Kucheto na Braun*** = ***Browne 's dog***)

{ h3: proper_q_rel(x5, h4, h6),
h7: named_rel(x5, "Browne"),
h8: def_explicit_q_rel(x10, h9, h11),
h12: poss_rel(e13, x10, x5),
h12: dog_n_1_rel(x10) }

to

{ h3: na_p_1_rel(e5, x4, x6),
h7: named_rel(x6, "Braun"),
h8: exist_q_rel(x6, h9, h10),
h3: kuche_n_1_rel(x4),
h11: exist_q_rel(x4, h12, h13) }

Additionally, such correspondences might be equipped with similarity scores on the basis of word alignment types involved in the corresponding phrase, as well as the type of the phrase itself. For example, if the word alignment of two corresponding phrases involves only sure links, then the MRS alignment for these phrases also is assumed to be sure. Respectively, if on word level there are unsure links, then the MRS alignment could be assumed to be unsure. This idea could be developed further depending on the application. Also, in some cases the MRS level alignment could be assumed to be sure, although it includes some unsure links on word level. For example, in case of analytical verb forms many elements will be aligned only by possible links, but the whole forms are linked as a sure correspondence. We believe that such pairs of sentences with appropriate syntactic and semantic analyses and word alignment are a valuable source for construction of alignments on semantic level.

In our project, the mappings (explicit or inferred) are used for definition of a procedure for generating transfer rules as outlined in the introductory section.

5 Conclusion

In this paper we presented the alignment strategies behind the Bulgarian-English parallel treebank. The focus was on word and MRS level. On the base of each word alignment, an MRS alignment is produced together with the corresponding elementary predicates.

Although the current interannotator agreement on the word level is promising - 92 %, we will continue with the development of the guidelines in parallel to the alignment process.

The language specific features, which are likely to influence the transfer of information from Bulgarian to English, are as follows:

- Similarly to English and in contrast to other Slavic languages, Bulgarian is analytic language with a well-developed temporal system;
- Unlike English and similarly to other Slavic languages, Bulgarian has a relatively free word order and is a pro-drop language;
- Like other Slavic languages, Bulgarian verbs encode the aspect lexically;
- Being part of the Balkan Sprachbund, Bulgarian has clitics and clitic reduplication;
- Like other Slavic languages, Bulgarian has a double negation mechanism;
- Bulgarian polar questions are formed with a special question particle, which has also a foculizing role;
- Like other Slavic languages, the modification is mostly done by the adjectives (garden dog (EN) vs. gradinsko kuche (BG, 'garden-adjective dog')).

We hope that the MRS alignment in the treebank provides a good abstraction over the language specific features of Bulgarian as well as adequate equivalences to the English linguistic phenomena.

Acknowledgments

This work has been supported by the European project EuroMatrixPlus (IST-231720).

References

Ahrenberg L., Merkel M., Hein A.S., Tiedemann J. 2000. *Evaluation of Word Alignment Systems*. In: Proc. of the 2nd International Conference on Linguistic Resources and Evaluation (LREC). Athens, Greece, Vol. III: pp. 1255–1261.

Bond F., Oepen S., Nichols E., Flickinger D., Velldal E. and Haugereid P. 2011 (to appear). Deep open source machine translation. In Machine Translation Journal.

Copestake A., Flickinger D., Pollard C., and Sag I. 2005. *Minimal Recursion Semantics: An Introduction*. Research on Language and Computation, 3(4), pp. 281–332.

Copestake A. and Flickinger D. 2000. Open source grammar development environment and broad-coverage English grammar using HPSG. In Proceedings of the 2nd International Conference on Language Resources and Evaluation, pp. 591–598.

Graça, J., Pardal J. P., Coheur L., Caserio D. 2008. *Multi-Language Word Alignments Annotation Guidelines (version 0.9)*. Spoken Language Systems Laboratory (L²F). May 25, 2008. http://www.inesc-id.pt/pt/indicadores/Ficheiros/4734.pdf

Kruijff-Korbayová I., Chvátalová K., and Postolache O. 2006. *Annotation Guidelines for Czech-English Word Alignment*. In: Proceedings of the Fifth Language Resources and Evaluation Conference (LREC). http://www.coli.uni-saarland.de/~korbay/Publications/lrec06align.pdf

Lambert P., De Gispert A., Banchs R., and Mariño, J. B. 2006. *Guidelines for Word Alignment Evaluation and Manual Alignment*. In: Language Resources and Evaluation 39: 267–285. http://www.springerlink.com/content/dg2x327940442t12/

Macken, L. 2010. *Annotation Guidelines for DutchEnglish Word Alignment*. Version 1.0. TR, Language and Translation Technology Team, Faculty of Translation Studies, University College Ghent. http://webs.hogent.be/~lmac139/publicaties/SubsententialAnnotationGuidelines.pdf

Melamed, D. 1998. *Annotation Style Guide for the Blinker Project*. Version 1.0.4. Philadelphia. http://repository.upenn.edu/ircs_reports/53/

Merkel, M. 1999. *Annotation Style Guide for the PLUG Link Annotator*. http://www.ida.liu.se/~magme/publications/pluglinkannot.pdf

Nivre J., Hall J., Nilsson J. 2006. *MaltParser: A data-driven parser-generator for dependency parsing*. In Proc. of LREC-2006, pp. 2216-2219.

Och F.J., Ney H. 2000. *A Comparison of Alignment Models for Statistical Machine Translation*. In: Proc. of the 18th Int. Conf. on Computational Linguistics. Saarbrucken, Germany, pp. 1086–1090.

Oepen, S. 2008. *The Transfer Formalism. General Purpose MRS Rewriting*. Technical Report LOGON Project. University of Oslo.

Simov, K. and Osenova, P. 2011. Towards Minimal Recursion Semantics over Bulgarian Dependency Parsing. In Proceedings of RANLP 2011.

Tinsley, J., Hearne, M. and Way, A. 2009. *Exploiting Parallel Treebanks to Improve Phrase-Based Statistical Machine Translation*.CICLing'09. 318-331.

Vèronis, J. 1998. *Arcade. Tagging guidelines for word alignment. Version 1.0.* http://aune.lpl.univ-aix.fr/projects/arcade/2nd/word/guide/index.html

Parallel Corpora in Aspectual Studies of Non-Aspect Languages

Maria Stambolieva
Laboratory for Language Technologies, New Bulgarian University
mstambolieva@nbu.bg

Abstract

The paper presents the first results, for Bulgarian and English, of a multilingual TransVerba project in progress at the NBU Laboratory for Language Technologies. The project explores the possibility to use Bulgarian translation equivalents in parallel corpora and translation memories as a metalanguage in assigning aspectual values to "non-aspect" language equivalents. The resulting subcorpora of Perfective Aspect and Imperfective Aspect units are then quantitatively analysed and concordanced to obtain parameters of aspectual build-up.

1 Aims of the investigation

At the time of the appearance of the first studies on Aspect in the early 20th century, this term (a calque from the all-Slavonic "vid"), was solely used for the description of a category typologically characterising Slavonic languages, setting them apart from "non-aspect" languages. After a century of aspectual studies, the term has undergone considerable widening of meaning and forms part, in modern linguistics, of the grammatical description of languages of different groups. Thus, "aspectual classes" are set out for Romance and Germanic languages; the English opposition "non-progressive-progressive" is called "Aspect"; even the category of Correlation is often described as a "Perfect Aspect".

Far from supporting cross-language investigations, foreign language teaching and translation, the shoving of different language phenomena in the same Aspect-bag is nothing but misleading and problem-raising. Bulgarian teachers of English who have tried to draw a parallel between Bulgarian and English Aspect to their pupils are well aware of the unsatisfactory results. Translators from Bulgarian to English and back, and their editors, point to Aspect as a major pitfall. Aspect is, again, the category where systems for automatic translation seem to offer the least help – Cf. the translation equivalents provided by Google Translate for a few English sentences:

1. He sang the song. – Toy izpya pesenta.(Perfective Aspect, Aorist)
2. He sang for an hour – ?Toy peeshe za edin chas. (Imperfective Aspect, Imperfect Tense)
3. They ate the sandwich. – *Te yade sandvich. (Imperfective Aspect, Aorist/Present?)
4. Did you eat the sandwich? – *Znaete li, yade sandvich? (???)

In what follows, I will try to:

- define the essence of Slavonic aspect and, in particular, aspect as expressed in the Bulgarian language – in an attempt to demonstrate why, and with respect to the expression of what semantic oppositions, Bulgarian can be used as a metalanguage in aspectual studies;
- contrast Bulgarian aspect to the aspectual system of English;
- demonstrate the possibilities of using parallel corpora and translation memories in the cross-language study of aspect and present first quantitative results of the computational analysis of the data, with parameters of English aspect construal.

2 The Slavonic Category of Aspect

Slavonic aspect is an ***equipollent*** lexico-grammatical category covering the entire verbal system and unambiguously defined in the Lexicon. The semantic basis of the opposition is the presence or absence of a bound ([+Bound] / [-Bound]) in the topological structure of a situation or, in other words, the +Event/-Event nature of the situation. Events and non-events in Slavonic languages define a small set of Situation Types, which, after lexical filling, result in a large number of 'Action Modes'.

Depending on their situation type, eventive verbs may mark one-bound or two-bound situations: *zapeya* ('start to sing') / *izpeya* ('sing from beginning to end'). One-bound verbs mark either the beginning of a situation or its end phase - compare *zapeya* above:

.... [..........

Fig. 1. One-bound situations with initial bound

and *dopeya* ('finish singing'):

Proceedings of Recent Advances in Natural Language Processing, pages 39–42,
Hissar, Bulgaria, 12-14 September 2011.

..........]..........

Fig. 2. One-bound situations with final bound

Two-bound situations can be minimal – *namigna* ('wink'), *padna* ('fall'), *otlepya* ('unglue'):

..........[X]..........

Fig. 3. Two-bound minimal situations

or extended: *procheta* ('read through'), *prepluvam* (swim through), *pospya* ('sleep a while'):

...........[XXX..]...........

Fig. 4. Two-bound extended situations

Non-Eventive verbs may mark s i m p l e non-bounded situations of the Action Modes Statal: *haresvam* ('like'), *imam* ('have'), *izglezhdam* ('seem', 'appear'), *cherveneya* ('be red), *mladeya* ('appear young') or Processual - *ticham* ('run'), *zreya* ('ripen'):

..........]XXX..[..........

Fig. 5. Simple noun-bounded situations

or else ***complex*** non-bounded situations: preparative situations, i.e. processes preceding an event - *zapyavam* ('be about to start singing'):

..........] [[X(XX..)]..........

Fig. 6. Complex non-bounded situations: Preparatives

and iterative situations, i.e. series of similar events – *kiham* ('sneeze'), *izpyavam* ('repeatedly sing'):

..........][X] [X] ([X]...)[..........

Fig. 7. Complex non-bounded situations: Iteratives.

Preparative and iterative situations are generally expressed by verbs which are derivatively (prefixally or suffixally) formed out of perfective verbs marking momentary or extended events.

The grammaticalisation of the opposition Non-Event/Event is a typological feature of Slavonic languages which sets them apart from languages of the Germanic and Romance groups. Further, in Slavonic languages the expression of aspectual information is concentrated in the verb. Hence, the presence of a perfective or imperfective verb defines unambiguously the aspectual value of the sentence.

Bulgarian stands out among Slavonic languages in that it manifests the Perfective-Imperfective opposition to the highest degree of regularity and grammaticalisation within the language group. As Yu. Maslov points out (Maslov 1984, p.97):

'It should not be thought that the principle of the positive suffixal expression of the Imperfective Aspect and the negative, null expression of the Perfective Aspect forms an exclusive feature of the Bulgarian language area [...] However, it is precisely in the Bulgarian language area that this principle has found its fullest and most consistent development. The specifics of the Bulgarian system in this respect [..] is not in the deviation from the Slavonic language type, but in the fullest expression of the developmental tendencies built in the Slavonic grammatical system [...].'

It is the regular, systematic character of the expression of the eventive/non-eventive nature of a situation in the verb and the richess of lexical verb types that defines the possibility to use Bulgarian as a metalanguage *sui generis* in aspectual studies.

3 Aspect Studies for the English Language

Even though Aspect forms part of the verbal categories claimed by English grammar, little -- if any -- of the defining features of the Slavonic category can be said to be applicable to the English data.

In harmony with the analysis of other non-aspect languages, aspectual studies of the English verb start with Verb Classes. A proliferation of classifications of these is in circulation, ranging from Aristotle's tripartition through Vendler (1957), Kenny (1963), Mourelatos (1981), Smith (1997), to name but a notable few. Surprisingly, not one of these classifications parallels the grammaticalised Slavonic opposition in distinguishing, first and foremost, events from non-events. Quite the reverse, the first line is, as a rule, drawn between states and processes. J.-P. Descles (1990) even goes as far as to claim a *topological* distinction between states as non-bounded situations against processes and events as bounded situations. Such verb classifications are not very helpful in event construal and cannot form the basis of cross-language parallels with Aspect languages.

Unlike other non-Aspect languages, the grammatical system of English does, in fact, incorporate an opposition of an aspectual type - the so-called "Progressive Aspect'. This is a *privative* opposition between an unmarked form and a marked form expressing non-boundedness, plus a large number of other components of meaning of a non-topological nature -- such as limited duration, irritation and other emotional colouring, increasing or decreasing activity, etc. The non-progressive form in the English "aspectual" opposition is *unmarked with respect to boundedness*. In other words, the English non-progressive verb cannot unambiguously define a situation as eventive or not. Seeing that, on average, English non-progressive forms occur approximately 20 times oftener than progressive ones in an English narrative text, this means that *English verbs are, largely, unmarked for boundedness*.

In his 1972 dissertation, Henk Verkuyl tried to demonstrated that in non-Aspect languages such as English, *events are construed*, i.e. boundedness obtains at VP and Sentence level as a result of the combination of verbs belonging to particular verb classes with quantified or unquantified complement or subject NPs. About the same time and independently of Verkuyl, M. Ridjanovic (1969) and A.Danchev, B. Alexieva (1974) in their English-Serbo-Croatian and English-Bulgarian contrastive studies, respectively, arrived at similar results, namely: aspect markers in English occupy a large stretch of the discourse. While Ridjanovic concentrated on the articled/non-articled noun phrases as major markers of Aspect, Danchev/Alexieva, processing a large parallel corpus (20 000 file-cards of English Simple Past Tense sentences and their Bulgarian equivalents!) arrived at a much greater variety of contextual markers. The authors ranked these as follows: adverbial phrases, verb semantics, subject phrase semantics, object quantification.

4 Parallel Corpora in the Aspectual Study of English

In view of the abundance of English-Bulgarian or Bulgarian-English parallel texts, (mainly in the form of TRADOS or Wordfast translation memories, but also simply aligned -- whether with tools for automatic alignment such as Win-Align or computer-assisted aligners such as MIX), the idea of using translation units and the aspectual values of the Bulgarian verbs to assign aspectual values to English sentences seems to make sense. While a wider-scope study based on a set of registers from a balanced corpus is the ultimate task of this project, the data presented below are drawn from a smaller parallel corpus of fiction texts. Even this corpus, however, clearly pinpoints lines of investigation and possibilities for applications of the approach.

The Bulgarian verbs in the parallel corpus were aspect-tagged with a choice of PA (perfective aspect) or IA (imperfective aspect) values. Translation units containing one or the other tag were asigned to one of three sub-corpora: an IAcorpus, a PA corpus and a "Mixed" corpus, with sentences containing both perfective and imperfective verbal forms. Each of the subcorpora was processed with the NBU BUILD segmentation programme, yielding quantitative information. At a next stage, concordancing was performed for larger segment identification.

Setting aside some 7% verbless setences, our corpus yielded the following quantitative information: appr. 31 % of the Bulgarian sentences contained Imperfective verbs only; appr. 23% of the sentences contained perfective verbs only; appr, 29% of the sentences contained both perfective and imperfective verbs, in different patterns.

4.1 Analysing the PA subcorpus

The analysis of the PA corpus quantitative data points to the following major PA markers in the English sentences:

Adverbial modifiers of time:

- *when* - upon concordancing, found to present, in about all cases, an instance of the relative adverbial, introducing a time clause;
- *then, now, now that, before, as* (=when), *eventually, finally, in+year* (e.g. *in 1984*), *at lunch, to begin with, the moment +subject+V.*

Coordination:

- *and* - as a coordinative link between event clauses;
- commas - Cf. above.

Lexical meaning of the verbs:

- communication verbs in the simple past tense, esp. *admitted, announced, insisted, lied, mumbled, prompted, said, thought (to myself), urged*;
- phrasal verbs: *drove away, went away, sat down*, etc.
- process verbs in the simple past tense.

4.2 Analysing the IA subcorpus

The following were found to be the major IA markers in the corpus:

Adverbial modifiers:

- temporal adverbials, e.g. *still*, *sometimes*, *repeatedly*, *when* (= *whenever*, closely followed by *would*), *as* (= *while*)
- *for*-phrases: e.g. *for a few minutes*;
- *do nothing but*, e.g. *We did nothing but quarrel*.
- adverbial modifiers of time containing NPs with attributes pointing to iterative situations, e.g. *every summer*.

Lexical meaning of the verb:

- link verbs, e.g. *was*, *seemed*, *grew*;
- extended state verbs, e.g. *know*, *hope*, *love*, *remember*.

Subject phrase semantics:

- Subjects semantically characterised as [-Animate], and esp. 'Inalienable property' subjects, e.g. *the symmetrical limbs*, *her expression*, etc. are systematically present in IA clauses.

4.3 Analysing the Mixed subcorpus

The most frequent patterns were found to be: IP (appr.9%), PI (appr. 4,5%), IPP and PPI (appr. 2.5% for each subtype). Typical factors defining the "mixed" status of the sentences are: complex verbal predicates, V + complement clause groups, presence of verbs of communication (typically Perfective), presence of verbs of thinking (typically Imperfective), Frame and Event situations. Conjunctions and complementizers, as markers of coordination and subordination, appear high in the rank list of most "mixed" subgroups.

5 Conclusions

The approach not only yielded results paralleling closely those of Danchev and Alexieva's corpus-based study (op. cit.) and the Stambolieva 2008 system-based one, but also contributed interesting additional information. Thus, coordination/compounding, of which no mention has ever been made in previous work, was found in the present study to occupy an important position in the hierarchy of English contextual PA markers. On the other hand, argument NP quantification was not found to hold the high-rank position predicted by Verkuyl (op. cit. and 1993). Concordancing elements of context occurring in both corpora - such as *when* - allows to arrive at structures which disambiguate them as PA or IA markers. Another important advantage of the approach is the possibility to obtain reliable quantitative information defining the hierarchy of units participating in IA or PA-marked predications. Above all, the specialised corpus thus obtained can be used as valuable translation memory or teaching aid.

References

J.-P. Descles. 1990. '*State, Event, Process and Topology*'. In: General Linguistics, vol. 29. No.3. Pennsylvania, pp. 159-200.

A, Kenny. 1963. *Action, Emotion and Will*. Routledge and Kegan Paul, London and New York.

Maslov 1984. Ю. С. Маслов. *Очерки по аспектологии*. Издательство Ленинградского университета, Ленинград.

Mourelatos A. Mourelatos. 1981. '*Events, Processes and States*'. In: Syntax and Semantics. Tense and Aspect, No.14. Philip Tedeschi, Annie Zaenen (eds.). Walter de Gruyter, Berlin and New York, pp. 191-212.

M. Stambolieva. 2008. *Building Up Aspect*. Peter Lang, Oxford, Bern, New York.

Z. Vendler. 1957. '*Verbs and Times*'. In: The Philosophical Review 66, 143-160.

H. Verkuyl. 1972. *On the Compositional Nature of the Aspects*. Reidel, Dordrecht.

H. Verkuyl. 1993. A Theory of Aspectuality. Cambridge Studies in Linguistics 1964. Cambridge University Press.

Coreference Annotator
A new annotation tool for aligned bilingual corpora

Mara Tsoumari
School of English
Faculty of Philosophy
Aristotle University of Thessaloniki
54 124, P.O. Box 58, Thessaloniki, Greece
mtsoum2@gmail.com, mara@optimum-services.com

Georgios Petasis
Software and Knowledge Engineering Laboratory
Institute of Informatics and Telecommunications
National Centre for Scientific Research (N.C.S.R.) "Demokritos"
GR-153 10, P.O. BOX 60228, Aghia Paraskevi, Athens, Greece
petasis@iit.demokritos.gr

Abstract

This paper presents the main features of an annotation tool, the Coreference Annotator, which manages bilingual corpora consisting of aligned texts that can be grouped in collections and subcollections according to their topics and discourse. The tool allows the manual annotation of certain linguistic items in the source text and their translation equivalent in the target text, by entering useful information about these items based on their context.

1 Introduction

The annotation tool, Coreference Annotator, has been developed within the framework of wider research in the analysis of parallel texts from a translation point of view. More specifically, the research attempts a theoretical classification of the translation of European Union texts in the light of Relevance Theory (Tsoumari, 2008), and examines a special use monodirectional bilingual corpus consisting of aligned English (originals/source texts) and Greek (translations/target texts) versions of press releases of the European Commission.

The aim of the annotation tool is for the researcher to trace and annotate manually certain linguistic items in the source text and their translation equivalent in the target text, by entering useful information about these items based on their context. The focus for this study is on identifying discourse markers and conjunctions that express concession/contrast/adversity in the source text and then locating their translation equivalent in the target text. To the group of markers mentioned above, the conjunction 'and' has been added. Cases of omission of source text conjunctions or discourse markers, or addition of conjunctions or discourse markers in the target text are also marked.

2 Motivation

The scope of the research that motivated the creation of this tool combines mainly translation, parallel corpora (original-source texts and translation-target texts), semantics, pragmatics, and discourse. A parallel aligned corpus of press releases of the European Commission is examined both translationally and linguistically to reach conclusions about how certain linguistic items are translated, potentially reflecting the intention of the authors; the expectations of the readers; whether intentionality and expectations change when moving from the source text to the target text; and effects from genre, discourses depending on the topics of the documents, public sentiment or culture.

2.1 Translation in the EU

There is an intriguing matter in the translation of European Union documents into all or some of the official languages of the European Union. On the one hand, there are rules and regulations governing the operation of European countries together as a whole, as a single unity forming the European Union, and EU culture and mentality. On the other hand, the European countries-member states maintain their national cultures and mentalities. Research has shown that the culture of the

Proceedings of Recent Advances in Natural Language Processing, pages 43–52,
Hissar, Bulgaria, 12-14 September 2011.

EU edifice is different from national cultures, has a culture of its own, despite the likely blurred borderlines between them (Koskinen, 2001; Koskinen, 2004). EU texts and their translation serve a primary communicative situation, since original texts are written to be translated so as to help EU (source text) authors reach different national (target) language users. Some of the characteristics of EU texts are that they are often produced and translated almost at the same time (Koutsivitis, 1994); translation may constitute the starting point to improve the 'original' (Koutsivitis, 2003); the writers are usually a group of people or a committee; most source texts are written in English and to a lesser degree in French and German (three procedural languages); the authors are not necessarily native speakers of the language they use for writing; source texts may not always be written in one language and have special linguistic, syntactical and stylistic characteristics called Eurojargon, Eurobabble or Eurospeak (Trosborg, 1997). Thus the translation process, strategies and methods are also affected by the particular circumstances of the production of target texts.

2.2 Press releases of the European Commission

EU press releases are one of the types of documents produced in the framework of the European Union and are distinct from non-EU press releases. The reason is that if we accept that the European Union has a culture of its own, as Koskinen (2001; Koskinen (2004) argues, then it is only normal to expect the production of EU culture-specific texts and genres. EC (European Commission) press releases are produced under the same EU-specific conditions as most EU documents are, i.e. multiple versions drafted and translated at the same time, non-native speakers drafting the documents etc. Culture has its own manner to construct and partition reality which is mirrored in its discourses, that is "modes of talking and thinking which can become ritualised" (Hatim and Mason, 1990). EU culture is no exception to that. In a corpus of aligned EC press releases an issue worth examining is whether the translation is affected by the different topics and discourses of the press releases.

2.3 Connectives: Relevance theory and Sentiment analysis

Connectives have been selected to be examined because they draw attention due to their status. According to Relevance Theory (Wilson and Sperber, 2002), the author produces his/her speech in such a way so that the reader will reach the speaker-intended interpretation with the least processing effort. The speaker, in order to achieve this, makes certain assumptions about the reader's background knowledge and, thus, expectations, and based on these assumptions formulates his/her discourse. From a relevance-theoretic perspective (Wilson and Sperber, 1993; Blakemore, 1987), connectives are not linking items, but devices whose meaning plays a part in the interpretation of an utterance. Among the different interpretations available, the hearer will decide which the speaker-intended one is, and connectives can facilitate the elimination of some of the available interpretations in order to achieve optimal relevance (Rouchota, 1998), i.e. the best possible interpretation for the hearer in terms of processing effort and effect.

Connectives have also been discussed in sentiment analysis. There is research which uses linguistic analysis and techniques to explore the sentiment of each sentence or phrase in a document. Meena and Prabhakar (2007) addressed the effects of conjunctions and sentence constructions in extracting sentiments associated with the phrases or sentences of reviews. Conjunctions are seen as crucial constituents when determining the polarity of a sentence. They found that, usually, either they alter the sentiment orientation to the opposite direction or they enhance the sentiment of the sentence.

Agarwal et al. (2008) involved in automatic sentiment analysis at sentence level in movie, car and book reviews observed that sentence structure has a fair contribution towards sentiment determination; conjunctions play a major role in defining the sentence structure. Their basic assumption is: "Not all phrases joined by a conjunct have same level of significance in overall sentiment determination".

3 Related tools

Parallel corpora are often used as linguistic resources in translation. Special tools have been designed to facilitate research in translation and multilingual parallel texts.

Callisto is a multilingual, multiplatform tool providing a set of “annotation services” (Day et al., 2004). Its standard components are textual annotation view and a configurable table display. Some of the tasks performed are automatic content extraction entity and relation detection, characterization and co-reference, temporal phrase normalization, named entity tagging, event and temporal expression tagging etc.

The IAMTC Project combines already existing facilities and newly developed ones and has developed an annotation tool for text manipulation. The Project involves the creation of multilingual parallel corpora with semantic annotation to be used in natural language applications (Farwell et al., 2008). Annotation includes dependency parsing, associating semantic concepts with lexical units, and assigning theta roles.

MULTEXT (Ide and Véronis, 1994) is a project involving the development of tools on the basis of "software reusability", and multilingual parallel corpora. It combines NLP and speech, and examines the possibilities for such a combination by harmonizing tools and methods from both areas. The annotation is performed with a segmenter, a morphological analyser, a part of speech disambiguator, an aligner, a prosody tagger, and post-editing tools. Thus, the annotated data provide information about syntax, morphology, prosody and the alignment of parallel texts.

Propbank is a project where a corpus is annotated with semantic roles for verb predicates (Choi et al., 2010). Annotation is performed with the help of Jubilee by simultaneously presenting syntactic and semantic information. The process is facilitated by Cornerstone, a user-friendly xml editor, customized to allow frame authors to create and edit frameset files.

Finally, there is ParaConc (Barlow, 2002) whose main characteristics are an alignment function, concordance search, search for specific words and their possible translations, corpus frequency and collocate frequency. But the tool has no annotating function.

These tools cannot fully meet the particularities of this research for the reasons discussed next.

4 Need for a new tool

The underlying factor that can bring the above different aspects and approaches together is an annotation tool that features certain specific characteristics that are hard to find all in one annotation tool. Coreference Annotator has those characteristics. In particular, a) uploading aligned texts already processed in an efficient alignment tool so as to achieve maximum alignment performance. The tool's ability to have as input aligned documents allows a corpus builder to use a reliable external aligner of one's own choice and then use the annotation scheme for the manual annotation of the aligned corpus; b) depicting the aligned texts in such an arrangement that each pair of aligned texts is clearly separated from the other pairs of aligned texts; each translation unit consisting of the source text segment and the target text segment in each pair of aligned texts is clearly and easily detectable from the other translation units. At the same time, it keeps its place in the text manifesting coherence and flow of text meaning in each language; c) allowing the location of possible translation equivalents in context of the instances of the linguistic items examined, always keeping the source text item and its target text equivalent in a close, binary relationship. This unfolds the variety of equivalents an item can have that may be either context dependent or context independent, and also highlights translation procedures and strategies; d) allowing the creation of a comparable profile at sentence level of the source text entry and the target text equivalent entry by entering accompanying information based on their context (distribution of the entries, collocations etc.) in the appropriate sections and fields of attributes – the source text entry and its equivalent text entry are seen comprehensively as a whole; e) displaying all the attribute sections and fields for each source text entry and its target text equivalent with one click to provide easy access which is important due to the large amount of data; f) allowing the examination of the target text in its own right to identify the cases, if any, of linguistic items under investigation that are present in the target text without being a translation equivalent of a source text entry; the annotation tool also provides for the creation of a profile for each target text addition entry; g) allowing the correlation of discourse topics with the frequency of the linguistic items and their translation equivalents in the two languages, and also with their microenvironments, thanks to the arrangement of the aligned texts; h) allowing the correlation of discourse topics, the frequency of the linguistic items and their translation equivalents, and the frequency of the items added in the target text; i) providing statistics based on the relationship of the source text entry and its target text equivalent where each result is fully and directly traceable in the corpus not only in terms of which pair of aligned texts it is found in but also in terms of its exact location in the pair, thus keeping track of text meaning and structure, and discourse; j) providing detailed statistics which allows the grouping of information of the profile of the entries for specialized analysis of results; k) producing tables of statistics exportable to widely commercial formats e.g. excel for further processing, e.g. SPSS. Such a sophisticated annotation tool allows multidisciplinary analysis. Finally, the tool has been implemented as a component of the Ellogon language engineering platform (Petasis et al., 2002), making extensive use of its infrastructure for the easy creation of annotation tools.

5 Corpus of Collections

This tool has been tested with a corpus of English-Greek press releases issued by the European Commission from 1/1/2007 to 1/1/2009. The corpus was drawn from the electronic text library of all EU press releases (RAPID)[1]. The criteria for text selection of that corpus are the availability of a Greek version and the currency of topics. The corpus consists of three thematic collections: the Environment, Agriculture, and Presidency Conclusions, which are further subdivided into thematic subcollections within each collection to make transparent the different discourses. The corpus has been aligned using the WinAlign alignment tool – an application of the SDL Trados 2007 suite. Exporting the aligned corpus in plain text format made it an appropriate input for the annotation tool which has been adapted to accommodate such input. The use of a long-standing professional alignment tool aims at achieving effective performance in the segmentation of the parallel texts at the level of equivalent sentences or text segments, i.e. translation units (SDL, 2007).

6 Annotation scheme

Annotation is conducted by associating attributes to the linguistic items. The annotation tool contains three sections of attribute fields. The first section is general and the most frequently used. In the first section, the focus is on the source text entry (ST EN) and the target text entry (TT EL) where the latter is considered the translation equivalent of the former in that context. The ST EN fields that follow relate to accompanying information of that token based on the particular context. The same goes for the TT EL fields. The next section, TT Addition, involves the addition of the items in question in the target texts. The third section, Context, involves the context of the texts. The original concept of that section is an attempt to map the differences emerging from the translation process between the two texts. There is great flexibility in designing the annotation scheme since using xml language allows the creation of different attributes and values or sections of attributes or the change of the existing attributes and values or sections of attributes.

6.1 Toolbar

The toolbar is on the top of the screen (see Figure 1) where the collections and the filenames of the aligned documents of each collection are found. The arrow icons guide the annotator to the next or previous document of the collection. Few more icons facilitate managing the documents.

After selecting a collection and an aligned document, on the left side of the tool we can see the document in an aligned form – one column with the source text (ST) and one column with the target text (TT). The aligned document is presented in translation units, i.e. linked source and target text segments, with serial numbers for each unit for easier reference/retrieval when analysing a corpus. Also, to facilitate the visual separation of the translation units the background colour of the units alternates between white and light blue.

6.2 First section of attributes – General

On the right side of the tool, the three sections of attributes are presented. In the first section, the focus is on the source text entry (ST EN) and the target text entry (TT EL) where the latter is considered the translation equivalent of the former in that context. The ST EN and TT EL fields that follow relate to accompanying information of those tokens based on the particular context. When there is an arrow icon on the fields, there is a drop-down list of attributes to select. When an item is annotated the tool highlights it. Different annotated entries are highlighted with different colours but each ST EN entry has the same colour with its TT

[1] http://europa.eu/rapid/searchAction.do

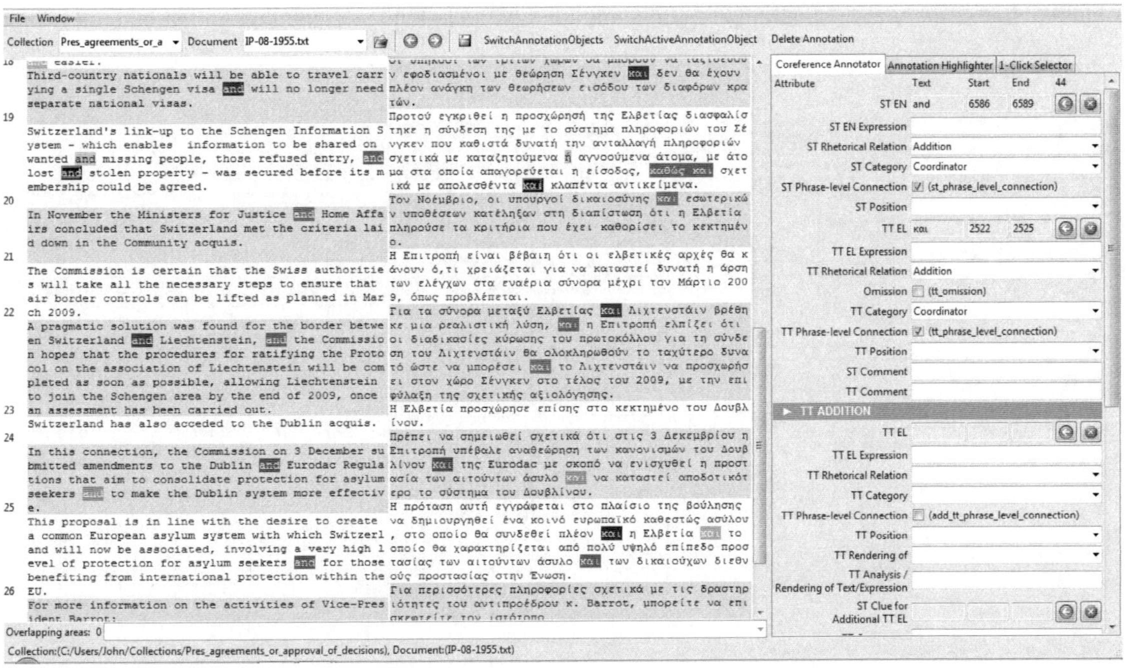

Figure 1: Toolbar and first section of Coreference Annotator – General.

EL equivalent entry. The fields ST EN/TT EL Expression accommodate cases where the ST EN/TT EL entries are part of an expression or form a collocation with the surrounding words. Each entry is also annotated for its rhetorical relation and category in that particular context. The values in these fields have been selected in relation to the connectives and discourse markers of interest. For cases where the discourse marker or connective has another function besides the linking one, the value "0" in the ST/TT Rhetorical Relation fields and the value "Other" in the ST/TT Category fields have been provided. There is also provision if a punctuation mark is in place of a TT EL entry. The checkbox of the ST/TT Phrase-level connection provides information about how often the ST and TT markers/connectives in question link predicates or non-predicates (noun phrases, adjectival phrases etc.) in their language respectively. Difference in the type of connection between the ST EN entry and its TT EL equivalent entry manifests different syntactic structures, and perhaps participant roles in the source and target languages. This in turn may reflect translation strategies e.g. shifts, transpositions, modulations etc. The ST/TT Position fields relate to the distribution of the tokens. When the ST EN entry and its TT EL equivalent are seen in parallel and a change in position is noted, then different thematic and rhematic structures, and focus may be reflected in the two languages. Omission of an ST EN entry in the target text is also checked. The last two fields, "ST Comment" and "TT Comment", allow comments by the annotator of the corpus that can be used either in revising or in analysing the corpus annotation.

An example can be a token of the additive conjunction 'and' (see Figure 1): This entry involves the token 'and', highlighted with blue colour in the translation unit 20. Based on its attributes, it is a conjunction of addition (ST Rhetorical Relation = "Addition"), a coordinator in particular (ST Category = "Coordinator"), and connects phrases (non-predicates) ("ST Phrase-level Connection" box checked). The token acting as its equivalent in the target text is και (kae) 'and', which is also a conjunction of addition (TT Rhetorical Relation = "Addition"), a coordinator (TT Category = "Coordinator"), and connects non-predicates ("TT Phrase-level Connection" box checked).

6.3 Second section of attributes – TT Addition

The next section, TT Addition, involves the addition of the items in question in the target texts (see Figure 2 – TT Addition). There are similar fields

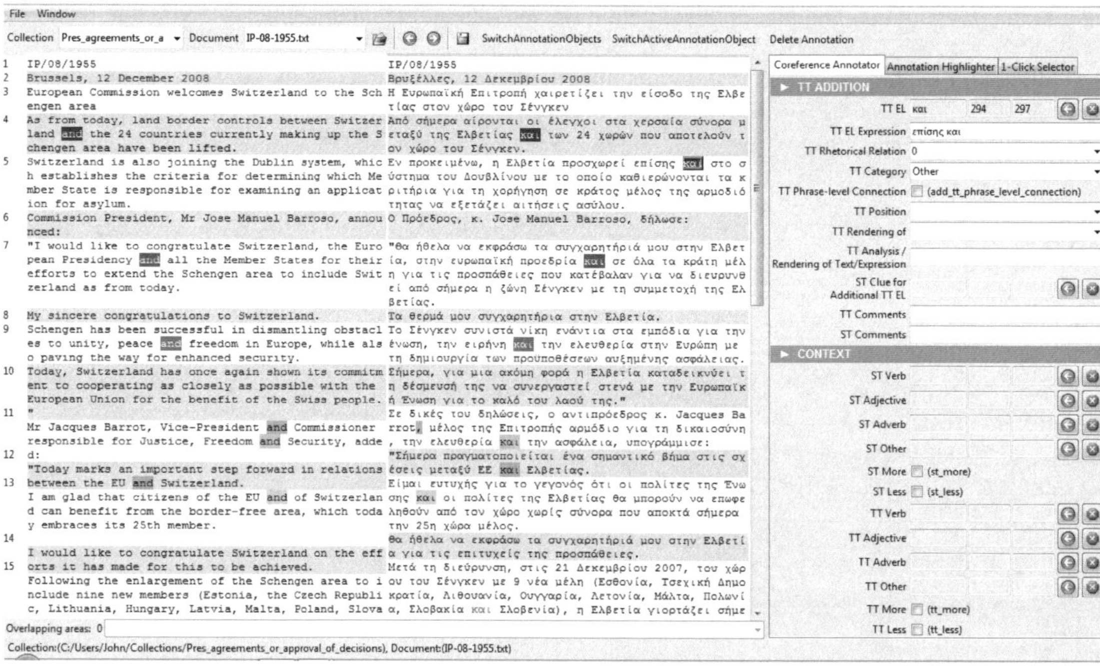

Figure 2: TT Addition.

as in the first section of attributes. Because in this section of attributes the starting point is the target text, a couple of extra fields of attributes have been added: the "TT Rendering of" field which attempts to classify the category of the word/phrase in the ST, if any, that motivated the addition of the discourse marker/connective in the TT; the "TT Analysis/Rendering of Text/Expression" field where the ST word/phrase is entered. Finally, there is one more field, ST Clue for Additional TT EL. Practically, this and the previous field have a similar function. An example can be found in translation unit 5 (see Figure 2): According to the annotation, the TT EL entry και (kae) 'and' was added in translation unit 5, is not used as a conjunction (TT Rhetorical Relation=0) and performs a different function from coordination in the structure of the sentence (TT Category=Other).

6.4 Third section – Context

The third section involves the context of the texts (see Figure 3). The original concept of that section is an attempt to map the differences that emerge from the translation process. These differences can be grammatical e.g. a change in the tense of a verb form, semantic e.g. the choice of a slightly/a lot different semantically TT EL equivalent, pragmatic e.g. the choice of a completely different expression in the TT to render ST meaning, or lexical e.g. the addition or omission of a word/phrase in one of the two texts. The following pairs of fields have been designed: ST Verb (or verb phrase) – TT Verb (or verb phrase), ST Adjective (or adjectival phrase) – TT Adjective (or adjectival phrase), ST Adverb (or adverbial phrase) – TT Adverb (or adverbial phrase), ST Other – TT Other. The last pair involves differences that do not fall under any of the other pairs. Then the differences recorded can be evaluated compared with each other based on which of the two options – ST option or TT option – is more or less strong in meaning, more or less informative, more or less appellative, and more or less affective. Some of these differences between the two texts are mandatory driven by language restrictions, for instance, or optional driven by cultural preferences, register, politics etc. Either way, these differences create an effect to the reader. So under the ST fields there are two checkboxes ST More, ST Less and under the TT fields respectively TT More, TT Less. For each difference entered the relevant box is checked; ST entry evaluated as ST More or ST Less and TT equivalent evaluated as TT More or TT Less. There is one last checkbox in this section, Compensation, called after the translation strategy. Compensation refers to making up for the loss of meaning

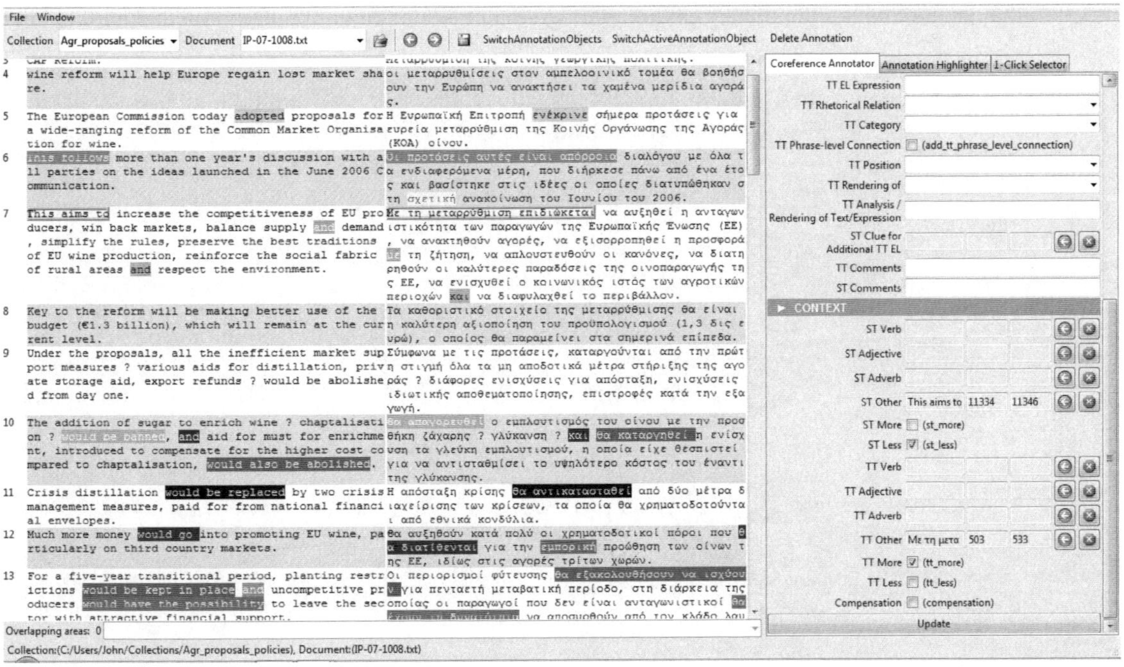

Figure 3: Context.

or effect in some part of the sentence in another part of that sentence or in a contiguous sentence (Newmark, 1988). This box is checked when the difference in context in the two texts is due to the translation strategy of compensation.

An example can be in translation unit 7 (see Figure 4): According to the annotation, the ST phrase 'This aims to' in translation unit 7, entered in the ST Other field is classified as ST Less compared to its TT equivalent phrase Με τη μεταρρύθμιση επιδιώκεται (Mae ti metarythmisi epidioketai) 'With the reform it is aimed'. The reason is the act of referring in the English segment where the demonstrative pronoun 'This', a lexicalized deictic element or indexical, is clarified in the Greek segment with the nominal referent μεταρρύθμιση (metarythmisi) 'reform'. So the TT phrase is more informative than the ST phrase. Because the foregrounded nominal in the TT phrase Με τη μεταρρύθμιση (Mae ti metarythmisi epidioketai) 'With the reform it is aimed' refers to the pronominal fronted in the ST, this is another factor which enhances the effect of the referring act in relation to the transposition between active and passive voice. Thus, the referring act prevails and classifies the TT phrase as TT More.

7 Statistics

Detailed statistics tables are produced covering all possible search criteria. The findings are easily traceable in the corpus in terms of collection, aligned text and position of the translation unit where the item is found in the aligned text. In particular, three tables are generated. The first table (see Figure 4) presents all the source text tokens of interest per aligned document and collection, their frequency, their translation equivalents along with their own frequency, and cases of omission of the source text connectives/discourse markers in the target text. At the end of each collection, there is the subtotal of the frequency of source text connectives/discourse markers and their translation equivalents. After all the collections have been examined the table presents the total results of the total of collections. An important element is that next to each result there are the numbered translation units where the source text connective/discourse marker and its target text equivalent are found. This last feature allows easy retrieval of the translation unit, which ensures keeping track of text meaning and structure, and flow of discourse.

The second table (see Figure 5) presents grouped data based on the first section of at-

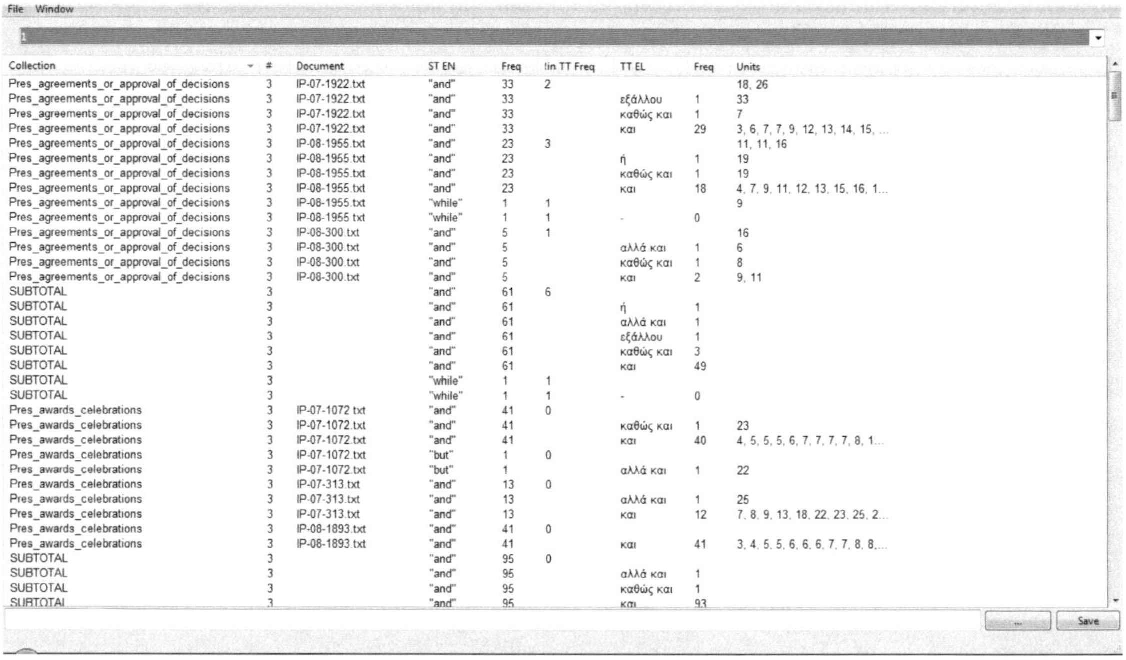

Collection	#	Document	ST EN	Freq	!in TT Freq	TT EL	Freq	Units
Pres_agreements_or_approval_of_decisions	3	IP-07-1922.txt	"and"	33	2			18, 26
Pres_agreements_or_approval_of_decisions	3	IP-07-1922.txt	"and"	33		εξάλλου	1	33
Pres_agreements_or_approval_of_decisions	3	IP-07-1922.txt	"and"	33		καθώς και	1	7
Pres_agreements_or_approval_of_decisions	3	IP-07-1922.txt	"and"	33		και	29	3, 6, 7, 7, 9, 12, 13, 14, 15, ...
Pres_agreements_or_approval_of_decisions	3	IP-08-1955.txt	"and"	23	3			11, 11, 16
Pres_agreements_or_approval_of_decisions	3	IP-08-1955.txt	"and"	23		ή	1	19
Pres_agreements_or_approval_of_decisions	3	IP-08-1955.txt	"and"	23		καθώς και	1	19
Pres_agreements_or_approval_of_decisions	3	IP-08-1955.txt	"and"	23		και	18	4, 7, 9, 11, 12, 13, 15, 16, 1...
Pres_agreements_or_approval_of_decisions	3	IP-08-1955.txt	"while"	1	1			9
Pres_agreements_or_approval_of_decisions	3	IP-08-1955.txt	"while"	1	1	-	0	
Pres_agreements_or_approval_of_decisions	3	IP-08-300.txt	"and"	5	1			16
Pres_agreements_or_approval_of_decisions	3	IP-08-300.txt	"and"	5		αλλά και	1	6
Pres_agreements_or_approval_of_decisions	3	IP-08-300.txt	"and"	5		καθώς και	1	8
Pres_agreements_or_approval_of_decisions	3	IP-08-300.txt	"and"	5		και	2	9, 11
SUBTOTAL	3		"and"	61	6			
SUBTOTAL	3		"and"	61		ή	1	
SUBTOTAL	3		"and"	61		αλλά και	1	
SUBTOTAL	3		"and"	61		εξάλλου	1	
SUBTOTAL	3		"and"	61		καθώς και	3	
SUBTOTAL	3		"and"	61		και	49	
SUBTOTAL	3		"while"	1	1			
SUBTOTAL	3		"while"	1	1	-	0	
Pres_awards_celebrations	3	IP-07-1072.txt	"and"	41	0			
Pres_awards_celebrations	3	IP-07-1072.txt	"and"	41		καθώς και	1	23
Pres_awards_celebrations	3	IP-07-1072.txt	"and"	41		και	40	4, 5, 5, 5, 6, 7, 7, 7, 7, 8, 1...
Pres_awards_celebrations	3	IP-07-1072.txt	"but"	1	0			
Pres_awards_celebrations	3	IP-07-1072.txt	"but"	1		αλλά και	1	22
Pres_awards_celebrations	3	IP-07-313.txt	"and"	13	0			
Pres_awards_celebrations	3	IP-07-313.txt	"and"	13		αλλά και	1	25
Pres_awards_celebrations	3	IP-07-313.txt	"and"	13		και	12	7, 8, 9, 13, 18, 22, 23, 25, 2...
Pres_awards_celebrations	3	IP-08-1893.txt	"and"	41	0			
Pres_awards_celebrations	3	IP-08-1893.txt	"and"	41		και	41	3, 4, 5, 5, 6, 6, 6, 7, 7, 8, 8,...
SUBTOTAL	3		"and"	95	0			
SUBTOTAL	3		"and"	95		αλλά και	1	
SUBTOTAL	3		"and"	95		καθώς και	1	
SUBTOTAL	3		"and"	95		και	93	

Figure 4: Statistics Table 1.

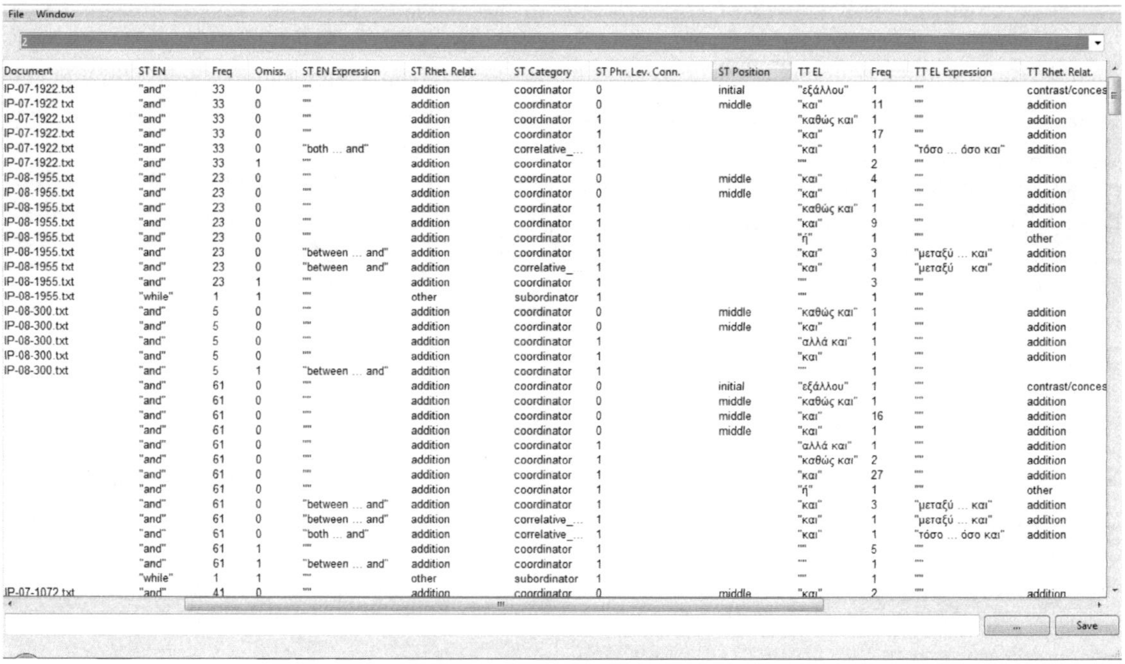

Document	ST EN	Freq	Omiss.	ST EN Expression	ST Rhet. Relat.	ST Category	ST Phr. Lev. Conn.	ST Position	TT EL	Freq	TT EL Expression	TT Rhet. Relat.
IP-07-1922.txt	"and"	33	0	""	addition	coordinator	0	initial	"εξάλλου"	1	""	contrast/conces
IP-07-1922.txt	"and"	33	0	""	addition	coordinator	0	middle	"και"	11	""	addition
IP-07-1922.txt	"and"	33	0	""	addition	coordinator	1		"καθώς και"	1	""	addition
IP-07-1922.txt	"and"	33	0	""	addition	coordinator	1		"και"	17	""	addition
IP-07-1922.txt	"and"	33	0	"both ... and"	addition	correlative_...	1		"και"	1	"τόσο ... όσο και"	addition
IP-07-1922.txt	"and"	33	1	""	addition	coordinator	1		""	2	""	
IP-08-1955.txt	"and"	23	0	""	addition	coordinator	0	middle	"και"	4	""	addition
IP-08-1955.txt	"and"	23	0	""	addition	coordinator	0	middle	"και"	1	""	addition
IP-08-1955.txt	"and"	23	0	""	addition	coordinator	1		"καθώς και"	1	""	addition
IP-08-1955.txt	"and"	23	0	""	addition	coordinator	1		"και"	9	""	addition
IP-08-1955.txt	"and"	23	0	""	addition	coordinator	1		"ή"	1	""	other
IP-08-1955.txt	"and"	23	0	"between ... and"	addition	coordinator	1		"και"	3	"μεταξύ ... και"	addition
IP-08-1955.txt	"and"	23	0	"between and"	addition	correlative_	1		"και"	1	"μεταξύ και"	addition
IP-08-1955.txt	"and"	23	1	""	addition	coordinator	1		""	3	""	
IP-08-1955.txt	"while"	1	1	""	other	subordinator	1		""	1	""	
IP-08-300.txt	"and"	5	0	""	addition	coordinator	0	middle	"καθώς και"	1	""	addition
IP-08-300.txt	"and"	5	0	""	addition	coordinator	0	middle	"και"	1	""	addition
IP-08-300.txt	"and"	5	0	""	addition	coordinator	1		"αλλά και"	1	""	addition
IP-08-300.txt	"and"	5	0	""	addition	coordinator	1		"και"	1	""	addition
IP-08-300.txt	"and"	5	1	"between ... and"	addition	coordinator	1		""	1	""	
	"and"	61	0	""	addition	coordinator	0	initial	"εξάλλου"	1	""	contrast/conces
	"and"	61	0	""	addition	coordinator	0	middle	"καθώς και"	1	""	addition
	"and"	61	0	""	addition	coordinator	0	middle	"και"	16	""	addition
	"and"	61	0	""	addition	coordinator	0	middle	"και"	1	""	addition
	"and"	61	0	""	addition	coordinator	1		"αλλά και"	1	""	addition
	"and"	61	0	""	addition	coordinator	1		"καθώς και"	2	""	addition
	"and"	61	0	""	addition	coordinator	1		"και"	27	""	addition
	"and"	61	0	""	addition	coordinator	1		"ή"	1	""	other
	"and"	61	0	"between ... and"	addition	coordinator	1		"και"	3	"μεταξύ ... και"	addition
	"and"	61	0	"between ... and"	addition	correlative_...	1		"και"	1	"μεταξύ ... και"	addition
	"and"	61	0	"both ... and"	addition	correlative_...	1		"και"	1	"τόσο ... όσο και"	addition
	"and"	61	1	""	addition	coordinator	1		""	5	""	
	"and"	61	1	"between ... and"	addition	coordinator	1		""	1	""	
	"while"	1	1	""	other	subordinator	1		""	1	""	
IP-07-1072.txt	"and"	41	0	""	addition	coordinator	0	middle	"και"	2	""	addition

Figure 5: Statistics Table 2.

tributes. It includes the elements of the first statistics table enriched with the accompanying attributes of both source and target text entries. The results present linearly, focusing on the ST entry – TT equivalent entry pair, the attributes which accompany the pair. Every time an attribute of the pair changes, there is a different entry in the results. Again, information on the document, collection and translation unit where the pairs with the specific attributes are found satisfies any search criteria.

The third statistics table involves results from the second section of attributes – TT Addition. It follows the rationale of statistics table 2 (Figure 5) but it focuses only on the target text items that have been added without being a translation equivalent of the source text items in question. Statistics for the third section of attributes about Context has not been designed yet because this section of attributes has not been fully tested in the corpus.

8 Conclusion

The Coreference Annotator is an annotation tool which is user friendly in its operation. It gives the researcher the advantage of selecting an external alignment tool for aligning a corpus of parallel texts according to his/her needs. It allows great flexibility in the study of various linguistic items and the translation process at the same time providing, therefore, multiple levels of analysis. Thus the researcher works with a tool that is easily adjustable to his/her varied needs in relation with the annotation of bilingual data.

References

Ritesh Agarwal, T V Prabhakar, and Sugato Chakrabarty. 2008. "I Know What You Feel": Analyzing the Role of Conjunctions in Automatic Sentiment Analysis. *GoTAL*, 5221(1):28–39.

Michael Barlow. 2002. ParaConc: concordance software for multilingual parallel corpora. In *Proceedings of the 3rd International Conference on Language Resources and Evaluation (LREC 2002)*, pages 20–24, Las Palmas, Canary Islands, Spain, May 29–31. European Language Resources Association.

Diana Blakemore. 1987. *Semantic constraints on relevance*. Blackwell.

Jinho D. Choi, Claire Bonial, and Martha Palmer. 2010. Multilingual propbank annotation tools: Cornerstone and jubilee. In *Proceedings of the NAACL HLT 2010 Demonstration Session*, HLT-DEMO '10, pages 13–16, Stroudsburg, PA, USA. Association for Computational Linguistics.

David Day, Chad McHenry, Robyn Kozierok, and Laurel Riek. 2004. Callisto : A configurable annotation workbench. In Maria Teresa Lino, Maria Francisca Xavier, Fatima Ferreira, Rute Costa, and Raquel Silva, editors, *Proceedings of the 4th International Conference on Language Resources and Evaluation (LREC) 2004*, pages 2073–2076, Lisbon, Portugal, 5. ELRA, European Language Resources Association.

D. Farwell, S. Helmreich, B. Dorr, R. Green, F. Reeder, K. Miller, L. Levin, T. Mitamura, E. Hovy, O. Rambow, N. Habash, and A. Siddharthan, 2008. *Interlingual Annotation of Multilingual Text Corpora and FrameNet*. Moutin de Gruyter, Berlin.

Basil Hatim and Ian Mason. 1990. *Discourse and the translator*. Language in social life series. Longman.

Nancy Ide and Jean Véronis. 1994. Multext: Multilingual text tools and corpora. In *Proceedings of the 15th conference on Computational linguistics - Volume 1*, COLING '94, pages 588–592, Stroudsburg, PA, USA. Association for Computational Linguistics.

Kaisa Koskinen. 2001. How to research EU translation? *Perspectives*, 9(4):293–300.

Kaisa Koskinen. 2004. Shared culture?: Reflections on recent trends in translation studies. *Target*, 16(1):143–156.

Vasilis Koutsivitis. 1994. *Theoria tis Metafrasis*. Ellinikes Panepistimiakes Ekdoseis, Athens, Greece.

Vasilis Koutsivitis. 2003. I proklisi tis polyglossias sti dievrimeni Evropaiki Enosi. In *Speech at the 4th Conference on Hellenic Language and Terminology, Athens*, Las Palmas, Canary Islands, Spain, October 30–31 and November 1st.

Arun Meena and T. V. Prabhakar. 2007. Sentence level sentiment analysis in the presence of conjuncts using linguistic analysis. In *Proceedings of the 29th European conference on IR research*, ECIR'07, pages 573–580, Berlin, Heidelberg. Springer-Verlag.

Peter Newmark. 1988. *A Textbook of Translation*. Prentice-Hall International, New York.

Georgios Petasis, Vangelis Karkaletsis, Georgios Paliouras, Ion Androutsopoulos, and Constantine D. Spyropoulos. 2002. Ellogon: A New Text Engineering Platform. In *Proceedings of the 3rd International Conference on Language Resources and Evaluation (LREC 2002)*, pages 72–78, Las Palmas, Canary Islands, Spain, May 29–31. European Language Resources Association.

Villy Rouchota. 1998. Connectives, coherence and relevance. In Villy Rouchota and Andreas H. Jucker, editors, *Current Issues in Relevance Theory, Pragmatics & Beyond New Series*, volume 58, pages 11–58. John Benjamins Publishing Company.

SDL International, 2007. *WinAlign User Guide 2007*.

Anna Trosborg, editor. 1997. *Text Typology and Translation*. Benjamins Translation Library, 26. John Benjamins, Philadelphia.

Mara Tsoumari. 2008. The translation of EU texts and relevance. In E. Walaszewska, M. Kisielewska-Krysiuk, A. Korzeniowska, and M. Grzegorzewska, editors, *Relevant Worlds: Current Perspectives on Language, Translation and Relevance Theory*, pages 188–205. Cambridge Scholars Publishing, Newcastle, UK.

Deirdre Wilson and Dan Sperber. 1993. Linguistic form and relevance. *Lingua*, 90.

Deirdre Wilson and Dan Sperber. 2002. Relevance theory. *UCL Working Papers. Linguistics*, 14.

Using Manual and Parallel Aligned Corpora for Machine Translation Services within an On-line Content Management System

Cristina Vertan
University of Hamburg
cristina.vertan@uni-hamburg.de

Monica Gavrila
University of Hamburg
gavrila@informatik.uni-hamburg.de

Abstract

Web content management systems (WCMSs) are a popular instrument for gathering, navigating and assessing information in environments such as Digital Libraries or e-Learning. Such environments are characterized not only through a critical amount of documents, but also by their domain heterogeneity, relative to format, domain or date of production, and their multilingual character. Methods from Information and Language Technology are the "plug-ins" necessary to any WCMS in order to ensure a proper functionality, given the features mentioned above. Among these "plug-ins", machine translation (MT) is a key component, which enables translation of meta-data and content either for the user or for other components of the WCMS (i.e. cross-lingual retrieval component). However, the MT task is extremely challenging and lacks frequently the availability of adequate training data. In this paper we will present a WCMS including machine translation, explain the related MT challenges, and discuss the employment of corpora as training material, which are manually and automatically parallel aligned.

1 Introduction

During the last couple of years, the number of applications which are entirely Web-based or offer at least some Web front-ends has grown dramatically. As a response to the need of managing all this data, a new type of systems appeared: the web-content management systems. In this article we will refer to this type of systems as WCMS. Existent WCMSs focus on storage of documents in databases and provide mostly full-text search functionalities. These types of systems have limited applicability, due to reasons such as the following:

- data available on-line is often multilingual;
- documents within a content management system (CMS) are semantically related (share some common knowledge or belong to similar topics).

Shortly, currently available CMSs do not exploit modern techniques from information technology like text mining, semantic web or machine translation.

The recently launched ICT PSP EU project ATLAS (Applied Technology for Language-Aided CMS[1]) aims to fill in this gap by providing three innovative Web services within a WCMS. These three Web services (i-Librarian, EUDocLib and i-Publisher) are not only thematically different, but also offer different levels of intelligent information processing.

The ATLAS WCMS makes use of state-of-the-art text technology methods in order to extract information and cluster documents according to a given hierarchy. A text summarization module and a machine translation engine, as well as a cross-lingual semantic search engine are embedded. The system is addressing for the moment seven languages (Bulgarian, Croatian, English, German, Greek, Polish and Romanian) from four different language families. However, the chosen framework allows additions of new languages at a later point.

Machine Translation is a key component of the ATLAS-WCMS and it will be embedded in all three services of the system. The development of the engine is particularly challenging as the translation should be used in different domains and on

[1] http://www.atlasproject.eu.

Proceedings of Recent Advances in Natural Language Processing, pages 53–58,
Hissar, Bulgaria, 12-14 September 2011.

different text-genres. Additionally, the considered language-pairs belong most of them to the lesser resourced group of languages, for which bilingual training and test material is available only in limited amount.

The availability of adequate and comparable training data for all language pairs in the ATLAS system played an important role in the architectural design of the MT-engine. The selection of training data was preceded by experiments on selected language pairs. Through these experiments we intended to investigate if small parallel corpora can be also used and with which implications on the translation quality. We investigated additionally the automatic (sentence) alignment in larger corpora in order to understand which implications alignment errors may have on the translation process.

In the following sections we report about our findings as follows: in Section 2 we present briefly the ATLAS functionality and describe the corresponding challenges for the machine translation engine. In section 3 we present the data we used for experiments and analyze it from the linguistic point of view. Section 4 deals with experiments which investigate the dependency between the amount of the training data and the translation quality. Section 5 gives an overview of future experiments and implementation steps.

2 MT-challenges in the ATLAS-System

2.1 The ATLAS-System

The core on-line service of the ATLAS platform is i-Publisher, a powerful Web-based instrument for creating, running and managing content-driven Web sites. It integrates language-based technologies to improve content navigation e.g. by interlinking documents based on extracted phrases, words and names, providing short summaries and suggested categorization concepts. Currently two different thematic content-driven Web sites are being built on top of ATLAS platform, using i-Publisher as content management layer: i-Librarian and EUDocLib. i-Librarian is intended to be a user-oriented web site which allows visitors to maintain a personal workspace for storing, sharing and publishing various types of documents and have them automatically categorized into appropriate subject categories, summarized and annotated with important words, phrases and names. EUDocLib is planned as a publicly acces-

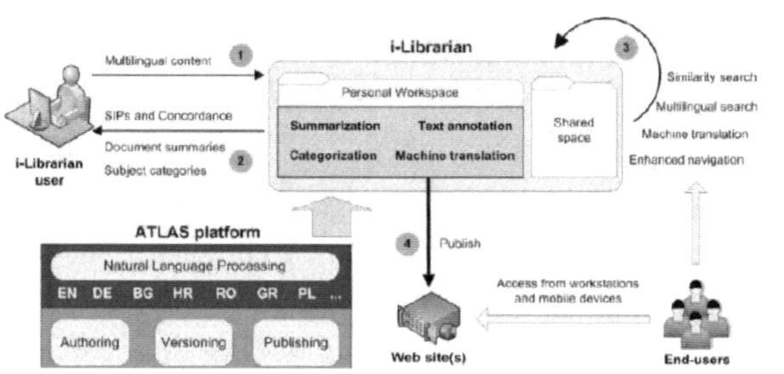

Figure 1: The iLibrarian Architecture

sible repository of EU legal documents from the EUR-Lex collection with enhanced navigation and multilingual access. All three services operate in the multilingual setting described in Section 1. To justify the need of embedded language technology tools within the ATLAS platform we detail here only the functionalities of i-Librarian.

The i-Librarian service (see Figure 2.1):

- addresses the needs of authors, students, young researchers and readers,
- gives the ability to easily create, organize and publish various types of documents,
- allows users to find similar documents in different languages, to share personal works with other people, and to locate the most essential texts from large collections of unfamiliar documents.

The facilities described above are supported through intelligent language technology components like automatic classification, named entity recognition and information extraction, automatic text summarization, machine translation and cross-lingual retrieval. These components are integrated into the system in a brick-like architecture, which means that each component is built on top of the other. The baseline brick is the language processing chains component which ensure a heterogeneous linguistic processing of all documents independent of their language (Ogrodniczuk, 2011). A processing chain for a given language includes a number of existing tools, adjusted and (or) fine-tuned to ensure their interoperability. In most respects a language processing chain does not require development of new software modules, but rather combining existing tools.

With respect to the machine translation engine the language processing tools provide the part-of-speech (PoS) annotation necessary for factored models and ensure named entity recognition. Other bricks of the ATLAS architecture feed information into the translation engine as follows:

1. the document categorization gives information about the domain of a particular document;

2. the automatic summarization deals with anaphora resolutions and pre-processes the document in order to simplify the translation task.

2.2 Challenges of the MT-Task

The machine translation (MT) engine is integrated in two distinct ways into the ATLAS platform:

- the MT-engine is serving as a translation aid tool for publishing multilingual content for i-Publisher. Text is submitted to the translation engine and the result is subject to the human post processing;

- for i-Librarian and EuDocLib, the MT-engine provides a translation for assimilation, which means that the user retrieving documents in different languages will use the engine in order to get a clue about the documents, and decide if he wants to store them. If the translation is considered as acceptable, it will be stored into a database.

The integration of a machine translation engine into a web based content management system, presents from the user point of view two main challenges:

- the user may retrieve documents from different domains. Domain adaptability is a major issue in machine translation, and in particular in corpus-based methods. Poor lexical coverage and false disambiguation are the main issues when translating documents out of the training domain;

- the user may retrieve documents from various time periods. As language changes over time, language technology tools developed for the modern languages do not work, or perform with higher error rate, on diachronic documents.

With the current available technology it is not possible to provide a translation system which is

	BG	DE	EN	GR	HR	PL	RO
BG		666 k	161 k+ 647 k	169 k+ 749 k	165 k	663 k	168 k+ 361 k
DE	ACQUIS		1581 k + 9 k + 1264 k+ 42 k	TBC + 9 k + 1132 k		9 k+ 1271 k+ 37 k	392 k+ 33 k
EN	SETIMES ACQUIS	EUROPARL EUConst ACQUIS PHP		980 k + 10 k+ 1083 k	150 k	10 k+ 1259 k+ 40 k	173 k+ 391 k+ 36 k
GR	SETIMES ACQUIS	EUROPARL Euconst ACQUIS	EUROPARL SETIMES EUConst ACQUIS		160 k	10 k + 1115 k	176 k+ 337 k
HR	SETIMES		SETIMES	SETIMES			176 k
PL	ACQUIS	EUConst ACQUIS PHP	EUConst ACQUIS PHP	EUConst ACQUIS			398 k+ 42 k
RO	SETIMES ACQUIS	ACQUIS PHP	SETIMES ACQUIS PHP	SETIMES ACQUIS	SETIMES	ACQUIS PHP	

Figure 2: Available parallel corpora for all language pairs within the ATLAS system.

domain and language variation independent and works for a couple of heterogeneous language pairs. Therefore our approach envisage a system of user guidance, so that the availability and the foreseen system-performance is transparent at any time.

From the development point of view the main challenge is provided by the high number of language pairs[2], most of them involving languages with rich morphology and belonging to structural different language families. For most of the language pairs a limited number of parallel aligned corpora are available. Additionally, the ATLAS platform should provide a basic comparable functionality for all language pair, so we cannot train models for different language pairs on completely different corpora.

After collecting information regarding parallel corpora for all involved language pairs, we decided to focus the development of basic training models on those summarized in Figure 2.2[3].

It can be observed that with exception of Croatian, for all other involved languages the JRC-Acquis[4] corpus offers a good training basis (coverage and size). In order to ensure domain portability we decided to train domain factored models as in (Niehues and Waibel, 2010). This approach allows the usage of small domain specific corpora. Small corpora have the advantage that they can be manually aligned, or at least manually corrected. In order to see how the translation engine behaves when exposed to large but automatically trained corpora and to small but manually aligned texts, we performed several analyses described in sec-

[2]More than 40 language-pairs.

[3]We do not consider in this table the recent additions from February 4th, 2011 concerning the Europarl corpus.

[4]`http://optima.jrc.it/Acquis/`.

tion 4.

3 Manually Aligned Small Corpora vs. Automatically Aligned Large Corpora

We decided to make selective experiments on corpora involving following language pairs: English, Romanian and German. Our choice is based on the availability of human evaluators speaking all three languages, but also by the fact that the languages belong to structural different families (Romania is in the Latin language family, English and German are Germanic languages). Additionally Romanian and German are highly inflected.

3.1 JRC-Acquis

The JRC-Acquis Communautaire is nowadays one of the mostly used parallel aligned corpus for training models in statistical machine translation (Koehn et al., 2009). We do not make here an extensive presentation of the SMT system but present in Table 1 and 2 just a comparative statistics on the three selected languages[5]. From these tables we can infer that the size of the training material has large variations across different language pairs within the JRC-Acquis.

Language pair	No. of documents	No. of links
German-Romanian	6558 docs	391972 links
German-English	23430 docs	1264043 links
English-Romanian	6557 docs	391334 links

Table 2: JRC-Acquis alignment statistics (docs=documents).

The corpus is automatically paragraph-aligned, where a paragraph is a simple or complex sentence or a sub-sentential phrase (such as noun-phrase).

3.2 RoGER

RoGER (Romanian German English, Russian) is a parallel corpus, manually aligned at sentence level. It is domain-restricted, as the texts are from a users' manual of an electronic device. The languages included in the development of this corpus are Romanian, English, German and Russian. The corpus was manually compiled. It is not annotated and diacritics are ignored. The corpus was manually verified: the translations and the (sentence) alignments were manually corrected.

The initial PDF-files of the manual were automatically transformed into text files (.RTF), where pictures were either left out (pictures around the text), or replaced with text (pictures inside the text). The initial text was preprocessed by replacing numbers, websites and images with "meta-notions" as follows: numbers by NUM, pictures by PICT and websites by WWWSITE. In order to simplify the translation process, some abbreviations were expanded. The sentences were manually aligned, first for groups of two languages. This way we obtained two alignment files. Finally, the two alignment files obtained were merged, so that, after all, RoGER contained all four languages. The merged text files are XML encoded, as shown below:

```
<?xml version=''1.0''
encoding=''UTF-8''?>
<sentences>
...............
<sentence id=''1010''>
<en>Press Options and some of the
following options may be available
.</en>
<de>Druecken Sie Optionen .  und
einige der folgenden Optionen sind ggf.
verfuegbar .</de>
<ro>Apasati Optiuni dupa care unele din
urmatoarele optiuni pot fi disponibile
.</ro>
<ru>...</ru>
</sentence>
.....................
</sentences>
```

The corpus contains 2333 sentences for each language. More statistical data about the corpus is presented in Table 3. The average sentence length is eleven tokens for English, Romanian and German and nine for Russian. Punctuation signs are considered tokens. More about the RoGER corpus can found in (Gavrila and Elita, 2006)

3.3 Linguistic Analysis of the Corpora

From both corpora we randomly extracted about 100 sentences, i.e. 100 sentences from the JRC-Acquis corpus for Romanian-English and 100 sentences from the RoGER corpus and the same language pair and direction of translation. These sentences were analyzed with respect to translation divergences and translation mismatches.

Translation divergence means that the same information appears in both SL and TL, but the structure of the sentence is different. Translation

[5]Information source: http://wt.jrc.it/lt/Acquis/JRC-Acquis.3.0/.

Language	No. texts	No. words (Text body)	No. words (Signatures)	No. words (Annexes)	Total no. words (Whole document)
German	23541	32059892	2542149	16327611	50929652
English	23545	34588383	3198766	17750761	55537910
Romanian (version 1)	6573	9186947	514296	11185842	20887085
Romanian (version 2)	19211	30832212	-	-	30832212

Table 1: JRC-Acquis statistics.

Feature	English	Romanian	German	Russian
No. tokens	26096	25850	27142	22383
Vocabulary size	2012	3104	3031	3883
Vocabulary (*Word-frequency higher than two*)	1231	1575	1698	1904

Table 3: Statistics on RoGER.

divergences are presented in the literature in (Dorr et al., 1999) and (Dorr, 1994). In the case of a translation mismatch the information that can be extracted from the SL and TL sentence is not the same. Translation mismatches have received less attention in the literature (Kameyama et al., 1991), but for corpus-based approaches they are important, as they directly influence the translation process.

Following translation challenges were observed within the JRC-Acquis:

- Divergences
  - Noun (NN) - adjective (Adj) inversion
  - Noun-Preposition-Noun (NN-prep-NN) translated as adjective-Noun (Adj- NN)
  - Subordinate clause translated as adjective
  - Different argument structure
  - Different type of articles
  - Voice change (for verbs)
- Mismatches
  - Extra information (the TL sentence is more explicit than the SL one)
  - Reformulations
- Wrong translation (due to incorrect alignment)

All these phenomena have a direct (negative) influence on the automatic evaluation scores. Although the corpus is domain restricted, the likelihood of at least one divergence or mismatch type occurring in a sentence is high. Only in approximately 10% of the sentences no phenomenon was encountered. As we encountered totally wrong translations in the corpus, it shows that the (paragraph-) alignments in JRC-Acquis are not always correct.

We also analyzed 100 sentences from the center of the RoGER corpus. We noticed that the diversity of the challenges is reduced, while the number of challenges is sometimes higher compared to what had been encountered in JRC-Acquis, with up to five challenges in an example (a sentence and its translation). Usually there is a one-to-one translation. Only in 12% of cases additional information appeared for one of the languages and in only 9% reformulations have been used. Two phenomena have been found most often: NN-prep-NN translated as NN-NN (or Adj-NN) and Adj-NN inversions.

3.4 JRC-Acquis vs. RoGER

The average number of challenges in JRC-Acquis (1.89 challenges per sentences) is lower than the average number in RoGER (2.20 challenges per sentence) for the languages analyzed. However, challenges with a more negative impact on the translation quality (such as “Wrong translation”or “Reformulations”) appear more frequently in JRC-Acquis. The phenomenon encountered more often for the language-pair analyzed is noun-adjective inversions.

4 Implications on the Design of the MT-Engine in ATLAS

The MT-Engine within the ATLAS System follows the hybrid approach combining a statistical based component and an example-based one. Both approaches are highly dependent from the quality and size of the training data The linguistic analysis above shows that both corpora present translation challenges which influence negative any further automatic processing. Therefore we argue that small domain specific corpora should be aligned manually at sentence level, or at least the alignment has to be checked manually.

Additional experiments presented in (Gavrila and Vertan., 2011) shown that using ROGER as training and test corpus, the performance of the system does not decrease dramatically. Our explanation relies on the linguistic observations in Section 3. The linguistic challenges are balanced by the manual alignment. In this way the corpus, although small has a more correct sentence alignment which triggers a more correct word alignment.

These experiments lead to the conclusion that for the ATLAS-System:

- JRC-Acquis will be used as basis training corpus, without making an manual corrections. This is impossible by the size of the corpus
- Small domain specific corpora will be first manually aligned at sentence level and afterwards injected in domain factored models.

5 Conclusion and Further Work

In this paper we described the integration of a machine translation engine within a WCMS system, dealing with a large number of less resourced languages. We investigated the linguistic characteristics of two parallel corpora and show how these influence the translation quality. Further work concerns a statistical relevant analysis of the linguistic phenomena presented in Section 3, involving other manually built corpora and other language-pairs.

Acknowledgments

The present work contains ideas from the ATLAS EU-Project, supported through the ICT-PSP-Programme of the EU-Commission (Topic "Multilingual Web")(Sections 2 and 4) and from Monica Gavrila's Ph.D research conducted at the University of Hamburg (Section 3).

References

Bonnie J. Dorr, Pamela W. Jordan, and John W. Benoit. 1999. A survey of current paradigms in machine translation. *Advances in Computers*, 49:2–68.

Bonnie J. Dorr. 1994. Machine translation divergences: A formal description and proposed solution. *Computational Linguistics*, 20(4):597–633, December.

Monica Gavrila and Natalia Elita. 2006. Roger - un corpus paralel aliniat. In *In Resurse Lingvistice şi Instrumente pentru Prelucrarea Limbii Române Workshop Proceedings*, pages 63–67, 63-67, December. Workshop held in November 2006, Publisher: Ed. Univ. Alexandru Ioan Cuza, ISBN: 978-973-703-208-9.

Monica Gavrila and Cristina Vertan. 2011. Training data in statistical machine translation - the more, the better? In *Proceedings of the RANLP-2011 Conference*, Hissar, Bulgaria, September.

Megumi Kameyama, Ryo Ochitani, and Stanley Peters. 1991. Resolving translation mismatches with information flow. In *Proceedings of the 29th annual meeting on Association for Computational Linguistics*, ACL '91, pages 193–200, Stroudsburg, PA, USA. Association for Computational Linguistics.

Philipp Koehn, Alexandra Birch, and Ralf Steinberger. 2009. 462 machine translation systems for europe. In *Proceedings of the MT Summit XII*, pages 65–72, Ottawa, Canada, August.

Jan Niehues and Alex Waibel. 2010. Domain adaptation in statistical machine translation using factored translation models. In *Proceedings of EAMT 2010*, Saint-Raphael.

Maciej Ogrodniczuk. 2011. I-publisher, i-librarian and eudoclib linguistic services for the web. In *Proceedings of the PALC 2011 Conference*.

Author Index